GYMNASTICS FOR THE BEGINNER:
A Coeducational Approach

BARRY L. JOHNSON
Texas A&I University at Corpus Christi

MARY JANE GARCIA
Corpus Christi I.S.D.

STERLING
SWIFT publishing company
p. o. box 188
manchaca, texas 78652

ISBN-0-88408-080-3

Second Printing

PREFACE

Gymnastics for students has reached an unparallelled status of popularity and value in physical education programs since its introduction into the United States in 1824. This is due in part to the fact that more educators now recognize the contribution of gymnastics toward the achievement of the major objectives of physical education. For example, gymnastics promotes: the development of such physical fitness components as strength, flexibility, muscular endurance, and cardiovascular endurance; an increase in the repertoire of a student's neuromuscular attributes such as agility, balance, kinesthetic perception, and reaction time; social development and an awareness of the need to follow safety rules; emotional satisfaction with opportunities for continued leisure enjoyment; and knowledge of the physical principles and physiological results of muscular activity. With the above potential values in mind, we can expect that gymnastics will continue to grow in importance as an adjunct to the achievement of the major objectives in programs of physical education.

While gymnastics has enjoyed considerable popularity in certain sections of the country, it is still struggling for a foothold in other areas. However, in Germany and other European nations, gymnastics is widely participated in and is considered a major sport. For example, in a recent gymnastic festival held in Germany, there were nearly three thousand competitors and approximately twenty-five thousand spectators.

Since the competitive sport of gymnastics is still unfamiliar to many students, who therefore lack appreciation for gymnastic exercise and interest in attending gymnastic programs, the authors felt that a book on gymnastics written for students could be instrumental in promoting interest in the sport and also serve as an aid to practical class activity. Thus, this book has been written primarily for beginning students, with emphasis on guiding them toward an appreciation of gymnastic exercise and knowledge of and interest in performance.

The book also includes information for new teachers of gymnastics. Other key features include descriptions of exercises to be done at home, interesting skills (described and illustrated), an emphasis on safety aspects, and the presentation of physical principles which represent the "why" of movement technique.

This book should not be misconstrued to be a complete book of beginner's gymnastics, for there are many other skills which could have been included. Moreover, skills deemed to be intermediate or advanced were purposefully omitted. However, over 100 skills are presented, and these represent comprehensive coverage for the beginner.

The intent of the authors in writing this book is:

1. To present elementary skills in those gymnastics events which are most often contested in the competitive sport.
2. To provide information helpful to beginning students in broadening their understanding and enjoyment of the sport of gymnastics.
3. To serve as a guide for teachers of beginning students.

It is sincerely hoped that this book will be instrumental in achieving the above goals.

ACKNOWLEDGMENTS

The authors wish to acknowledge their indebtedness to the following people for encouraging them and helping them gain the practical experience needed to write this book: Dr. John Piscopo, Dr. Gene Perkins, Mr. John Nipper, Dr. Ted Powers, Mr. Bill Bankhead, Mr. Vannie Edwards, and Jeanette Hawkins.

We also wish to express our appreciation to the many fine teachers in the various gymnastic clinics who have influenced our thinking concerning the "how and why" of gymnastics: Gene Wettstone, George Saupula, Charlie Pond, Dr. Newt Loken, George Nissen, Tom Maloney, Pat Yeager, Jerry Todd, Herb Loken, Frank Cumiskey, Sam Bailie, and members of the U.S. Olympic Gymnastic Teams who assisted at national and regional clinics during our days of training.

Special recognition should also be given to Dwight C. McLemore and Fred Martinez for assistance with illustrations and photographs and to our many students who served as "guinea pigs" for the stunts included in this book.

These acknowledgments would not be complete without a special note of thanks to Dr. D. Whitney Halladay, President; Dr. B. Alan Sugg, Vice President of Academic Affairs, and Dr. Ralph Gilchrist, Dean of Science and Technology, all of Texas A&I University at Corpus Christi, for their support during the writing of this book.

CONTENTS

PART I
Introduction

1

A BRIEF HISTORY OF GYMNASTICS

Some form of gymnastics was probably practiced even before the time of our earliest records. It seems reasonable to assume, for example, that while early man may have had a purpose in crossing from one side of a river to the other by means of a vine or pole, he also enjoyed the sensation of swinging, and from this he developed various acrobatic skills.

Ancient stone records and pictures indicate that balancing and tumbling were practiced in some form by the early peoples of China, Egypt, India, and Persia.

Records of early civilization in Greece show that gymnastics had a prominent place in the education of men. However, it is only fair to mention that gymnastics in those days referred to a variety of activities which we do not now consider to be gymnastics—for example, wrestling, boxing, and track and field. Even so, literature records that Greek soldiers practiced hand balancing prior to going into battle. There are also many accounts of acrobats performing various stunts, not only in ancient times in Greece, but also throughout other periods of history. Although the Greeks gave us the term *gymnastics,* many centuries passed before the term was used strictly to identify those activities now called gymnastics.

Germany was a major force in the development of modern gymnastics, producing many leaders who contributed greatly to the present system of gymnastics. The first teacher of organized school gymnastics was Johann Basedow (1723–1790). He believed that play and bodily exercise were important for normal growth and development of a child, and offered a wide program of activities including gymnastic exercise and lessons in balancing. Johann Pestalozzi (1746–1827) is considered the founder of free exercise. He developed a system of bodily exercises and arranged them according to difficulty and effect on the body.

The first book on gymnastics, *Gymnastics for Youth,* was written by Johann Friedrich Guts Muths. Guts Muths (1759–1839) served as a physical education teacher for fifty years and is now considered to be the "grandfather" of gymnastics.

He taught such skills as rope climbing, balancing, and a wide variety of stunts. While he believed that gymnastics had much to offer both boys and girls, he felt that girls should engage in a less strenuous form of gymnastics.

Gerhard Vieth (1763–1836), a strong believer in the values of gymnastics for students of all ages, is credited with developing many of the vaults, mounts, and dismounts which are still practiced today.

Friedrich Jahn (1778–1852), who invented the pommeled side horse, parallel bars, horizontal bar, and balance beam, is recognized as the "father" of gymnastics. He is also credited with founding the Turnverein (German Gymnastic Societies) which spread all over Germany and eventually to many cities in the United States.

Adolph Spiess (1810–1858) encouraged both the inclusion of gymnastics in the school curriculum and the participation of girls in the activity. It was through his efforts that gymnastics became a school subject in Switzerland and in Germany. Spiess placed considerable stress on gymnastic exhibitions as a means of holding the interest of students and also of selling his program to the public. Unlike Jahn, he devoted special attention to free exercise as a valuable event for girls and young children.

Gymnastic leaders from countries other than Germany also contributed to the development of gymnastics.

Francis Amoros (1770–1848) was a Spaniard who served as national director of gymnastics in France. He was probably the first to use the trapeze and rings as a form of gymnastics.

Franz Nachtegall (1777–1847) served as director of gymnastics for Denmark. He also directed the first recorded training school established to train gymnastics teachers.

Per Henrik Ling (1776–1839), a major figure in the evolution of Swedish gymnastics, developed a therapeutic and corrective system of gymnastics. He believed that gymnastics should be based on a thorough knowledge of the effects of the various exercises on the human body, and that gymnastics instructors should know the physiological and structural basis for each exercise they teach. His system was very formal, however, and contributed little to the competitive sport.

Archibald Maclaren (1820–1884) served as director of military gymnastics for Great Britain in the 1860s. He believed that the popular games of England could not produce a well-developed body without the inclusion of gymnastics. Practically all of Maclaren's followers were in the army and consequently made his program unpopular by formalizing it into a semblance of a military drill.

The development of gymnastics in the United States received its principal impetus from the German Turners who settled in this country. Dr. Charles Beck, a German, established the first program of German gymnastics in the United States in 1824. In 1826, Charles Follen, another German Turner, set up a gymnastic program at Harvard University and established the first gymnasium in the United States.

Because of political pressures, thousands of German citizens emigrated to the United States in the late 1840s. They established Turnverein Societies through-out the northern United States, and these societies promoted physical education by sponsoring outdoor games, gymnastic meets, and gymnastic exhibitions. The American Turners held the first national gymnastic meet in Philadelphia in 1851, with awards and honors bestowed on the victors.

In 1865, the Turners established The Normal College of the American Gym-nastic Union at Indianapolis for the purpose of training teachers of gymnastics. In the years which followed, they took advantage of every opportunity to sell their program of gymnastics to schools, and in many schools gymnastics became the physical education program.

In the 1880s, Amy Morris Homans and her associate, Mrs. Hemenway, pro-moted the growth of Swedish gymnastics by providing instructions for school-teachers.They also were instrumental in the establishment of the Boston Normal School of Gymnastics.

During the years between World Wars I and II, gymnastics was kept alive primarily through the efforts of the Turner Clubs, **YMCA,** Sokol Clubs, Swiss gym-nastic societies, and a few colleges and universities. School physical education pro-grams began to lean toward the lighter recreational types of activities. These popu-lar team games soon crowded gymnastics out of the programs, and as a result, the fitness and strength of Americans, particularly in their upper body regions, dropped to a new low. This became obvious from the records of men examined in Army induction centers of World War II.

During World War II, military leaders recognized the need for gymnastic activities in their physical training programs. This revival of gymnastics, coupled with the development of a new piece of popular gymnastic equipment called the Nissen Trampoline in 1939, influenced many schools to incorporate gymnastics in their physical education programs.

In Olympic Games competition, the United States has not fared well in recent years. In fact, it has not been since 1904 that the U.S. has won the un-official team title in the men's competition. At that time, Anton Heida led the men as they captured first place in every event. Then, in 1932, another strong team captured five gold medals but failed to score enough points for the team honors. In 1948, the U.S. women's team made their best showing with a third place win. Since 1952, Russia has dominated the competition for women, while Japan has set the pace in men's competition.

The growth of gymnastics in the United States has been rapid since 1950. With the advent of regional and national clinics, gymnasts from all sections of the country were brought closer together, sharing new ideas and stimulating greater competition. Television has brought into the homes of Americans the major competitions held throughout the world. Names of popular performers such as Olga Korbut, Nadia Comaneci, and Cathy Rigby are now common in family conversation. Further evidence of growth can be seen in the number of girls who attend and participate in the various clinics and meets held each year throughout the country. Also, an increasing number of girls are using gymnastic routines as their talent in nationally televised beauty pageants. Much of the popularity of women's gymnastics can be attributed to the untiring efforts of such people as Pat Yeager, Janet and Rudy Bachna, Vannie Edwards, Herb Loken, Muriel Grossfeld, and other teachers and coaches. Mr. and

*MISS LOUISIANA SEMIFINALIST PERFORMS GYMNASTIC ROUTINE
FOR TALENT COMPETITION*

Mrs. Glenn Sundby, editors and publishers of *The Modern Gymnast* and *Mademoiselle Gymnast,* have contributed greatly to the sport of gymnastics by disseminating national and international gymnastic news, photos, competition results, and instructions for men, women, and children.

At the beginning of the 1960s, a struggle for control of the sport of gymnastics, as well as other sports, developed between the Amateur Athletic Union and many of the collegiate coaches in the United States. The differences between the two groups led the gymnastics coaches to form their own organization, the United States Gymnastic Federation. Under the direction of Frank Bare, this organization has brought about a number of new and valuable changes in the sport. However, it is hoped by many followers of the sport that differences between the two groups can be settled amicably in the best interests of gymnastics.

Gymnastics has continued to grow at a rapid pace and has become more exciting with each passing year. Perhaps one of the greatest lessons we can learn from a history of gymnastics is that too much formality in our instructional programs can destroy the interest and fun which our students should derive from this activity.

2

GYMNASTIC WARM-UP AND DEVELOPMENTAL EXERCISES

Gymnastic Warm-Up Exercises

Before starting to learn stunts in the various gymnastic events, the beginner will find it beneficial to go through a series of light stretching exercises. These exercises are designed to increase flexibility and extensibility and to prepare the beginner for the more strenuous stunts ahead. The following exercises should be used at the beginning of each class or workout.

WRIST WARM-UP

Place the palm of the right hand against the inward side of the fingers of the left hand and press the fingers backward to extend or stretch the left wrist. After warming up the left wrist, perform the same movement against the right wrist. Wrist flexion and extension are extremely important for tumbling, balancing, and bar work.

6

Leg Extension Warm-Ups

With the feet slightly apart, lock the knees and bend downward, touching the floor with the fingers or palms of the hands for about ten repetitions. Leg extension in relation to the reach of the arms is especially important in free exercise and horizontal-bar work.

SHOULDER DISLOCATE

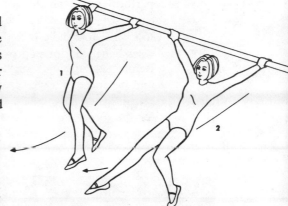

Standing with the back to a bar, reach to the rear and grasp the bar with a reverse grasp. Walk away from the bar until the shoulders roll or dislocate. Practice this movement, striving to get the hands closer and closer together. This exercise develops shoulder flexibility which is necessary for uneven bars, horizontal bar and rings.

This exercise may also be performed by grasping a rope or broom handle in front of the body, swinging the object upward and backward, and lowering it behind the back until the shoulders roll. The movement is then reversed and the object is brought in front of the body again.

Bridge-Ups

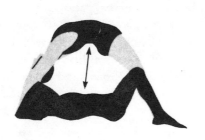

From a supine position on the floor, tilt the head back, arch the back, and walk the hands and feet as close together as possible. This exercise may also be executed by leaning backwards until contacting the wall and hand-walking down the wall until the hands and feet are on the floor. This exercise increases the flexibility of the back and shoulders which is important in tumbling and free exercise.

SPLITS

From a stand, extend the legs apart from front to rear or to opposite sides until the crotch is as near to the floor as possible. The splits exercise helps increase the range of movement for free exercise stunts and for straddle vaults to and from apparatus.

Developmental Exercises

Since gymnastics requires a trim and physically fit body for a better than average performance, each class or workout should be followed by a short period of special exercises designed for developmental purposes. Students who are overweight or too weak to handle their body weight satisfactorily should find the following exercises beneficial for improved performance of gymnastic stunts.

Rope Climb
(Boys and Men Only)

From a sitting position, climb hand over hand up a twenty foot rope. The beginner at first may have to use the feet, but, as his strength increases, he should use only the hands. This exercise is a good upper-body conditioner and increases the pulling power necessary for rings, parallel bars, and horizontal-bar work.

REVERSE AND REGULAR GRASP CHIN-UP
(Girls and Women Only)

The beginner should perform the reverse grasp chin-up on one day and the regular grasp chin-up the next day. The height of the bar should be adjusted to approximately breast level of the girl doing the exercise. The student grasps the bar, arms extended at full length, and walks under the bar until the body is at a 45 degree angle to the floor. From this position she raises the body to the bar and then lowers it to the former position. The performer should strive to perform 30 to 35 repetitions during each workout. This exercise overcomes weakness in the upper arms and enables the performer to execute pulling stunts in a satisfactory manner.

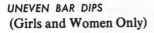

Handstand Push-Ups
(Boys and Men Only)

Kick up into a handstand against a wall and bend at the elbows, allowing the body to lower until the nose or forehead touches the floor. Push the body back to its original position by extending the elbows until they lock. The beginner should strive to work up to at least ten repetitions prior to completing his basic course. This exercise develops the pressing power of the body which is necessary for free exercise, rings, and parallel bars.

UNEVEN BAR DIPS
(Girls and Women Only)

From a straight-arm support on the low bar of the uneven bars, lower the body by bending the elbows until the angle formed is approximately 45 degrees. Push the body back to a straight-arm support by extending the elbows until they lock. This exercise overcomes weakness of the triceps. Work up to 8 to 10 repetitions.

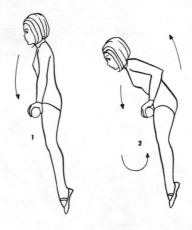

Dips
(Boys and Men Only)

From a straight-arm support between the parallel bars, lower the body by bending the elbows until a steady resistance is met in the shoulders. Push the body back to a straight-arm support by extending the elbows until they lock. This exercise develops the strength of the triceps. Work up to ten to twelve repetitions.

GYMNASTIC SIT-UP
(For Everyone)

From a supine position on a mat, bend at the waist and raise the upper body and the legs to a piked position. When the hands touch the shins, return to a supine position. Work up to 20 or 25 repetitions. This exercise overcomes weakness of the abdominal muscles and may decrease the size of the waistline.

ONE-HALF SQUAT JUMP
(Girls and Women Only)

The performer stands with the heel of the left foot even with the toes of the right foot. The hands are interlocked, palms down, and are held at the back of the head. From this position the gymnast lowers to a one-half squat position, immediately springs with both feet to an upright position above the floor while interchanging the feet, and returns to the half-squat position. This exercise is continued for 15 to 20 repetitions. The squat jumps should overcome weakness of the leg extensers.

Effects of Regular Exercise on the Human Body

Some of the effects of regular exercise (of a sufficient intensity and duration) on the human body that have been reported after careful experimentation are:

- improvement in cardiovascular endurance.
- increase in muscular strength.
- increase or decrease (depending upon the type of program) in the size of the body parts.
- increase in the number of capillaries in exercised muscles.
- ability to obtain greater explosive power (an increase in force during initial movement) for the improvement of performance.
- decrease in the formation of lactic acid resulting from exercise.
- a quicker return of pulse rate to normal following exercise.
- improvement in mechanical efficiency.
- removal, to some extent, of the inhibition to exert maximum effort in physical performance.
- improvement in speed of movement and reaction time.

Home Exercise

In an evaluation study, Kenny [2] found that exercising at home was the most popular form of maintaining physical fitness engaged in on an all-year basis by graduates of the University of Illinois. Since lack of time and facilities are limiting factors for many families, a quick workout at home represents the most practical approach to regular training or activity.

Among the exercises which may be executed within the limited space of most homes are:

. . . gymnastic warm-up exercises (wrist warm-ups, leg extensions, splits, bridge-ups, and shoulder dislocates) as described in this chapter.

. . . developmental exercises (squat jumps, gymnastic sit-ups, dips, and reverse and regular grasp chin-ups) as described in this chapter. The dips may be executed between two chairs, and the chin-ups may be executed on the closet clothes bar if a board with a notch in the upper end is inserted under the bar for added support. The knees and hips may be bent during the execution of such exercises when there is inadequate height between the floor and the point of support.

. . . balance stunts (tip-up, headstand, forearm balance, "V" seat position, and front and side scales) as described in **Chapter 3.**

. . . isometric exercises (numerous exercises may be performed within a limited space with an inexpensive isometric scale illustrated in this chapter). Many such exercises have been described and illustrated by Drury.[3]

. . . isotonic exercises (numerous exercises may be performed within a limited space with barbells and dumbbells). Such equipment can be stored under one's bed.

If students develop a knowledge and appreciation of gymnastic skills and exercises in college, they will be more apt to continue to use them after they leave school.

References

1. Johnson, Barry L., "A Comparison of Isometric and Isotonic Exercises Upon the Improvement of Velocity and Distance as Measured by a Vertical Rope Climb Test." Baton Rouge, La.: Louisiana State University, January, 1964. Unpublished study.
2. Kenny, Harold E., "An Evaluative Study of the Required Physical Education Program for Men at the University of Illinois." *59th Annual Proceedings of the CPEA*, Urbana, Ill., 1956.
3. Drury, Francis A., *Strength Through Measurement*. Marion, Ind.: Coach's Sporting Goods Corporation, 1963.

PART II
Events for Everyone

3

FREE EXERCISE SKILLS

The stunts presented in this chapter are frequently used in basic-tumbling and free-exercise routines. Many of the stunts are of a tumbling nature while others may be characterized as balance, flexibility, or strength stunts. Because of their varied nature, the stunts are not necessarily presented in a simple-to-complex sequence. In free-exercise stunts, the authors believe that teacher and pupils should plan their own progression in accordance with their interests, needs, and abilities.

14

TUMBLING SKILLS

FORWARD ROLL

From a standing position, bend forward and place the hands on the mat, duck the head forward, push the hips over the head, and bend the elbows, lowering the upper back to the mat while bending at the hips and the knees. As the upper back contacts the mat, grasp the shins with the hands and pull as *you roll down the back* and (from upper back to lower back) onto the buttocks and then onto the feet. If the back of the head or neck is allowed to contact the mat, this should be done in a gentle and controlled manner. Be sure and place your emphasis on learning one good forward roll and not a series of fast rolls executed with poor technique.

Safety. The performer should concentrate on keeping the body weight primarily on the hands and arms, while lowering gently onto the upper back during the roll.

Shoulder Roll

From a stand with the right leg a pace ahead of the left leg, bend forward looking between the legs and lower onto the right forearm. Push with the feet and roll over the right shoulder and diagonally across the back and onto the left hip. Keep the legs spread apart and as you roll onto the left hip, bend the left leg at the knee so that you roll onto the left knee, push with left hand, and step out on the right foot returning to a standing position. This stunt may be executed over either the left or right shoulder.

BACKWARD ROLL

From a sitting position, the performer rolls backward onto the upper back, placing the hands on the mat with the thumbs next to the ears while keeping the legs straight and the hips flexed. As the body weight is shifted onto the hands, the performer pushes with the arms, looks upward and moves the head back, and extends the hips into an arched position. Passing through a momentary handstand, the performer may either snap down to the feet or step down one foot at a time.

Safety. During the first few attempts, a spotter should kneel on both knees at the performer's left side, cupping the fingers of the right hand over the top of the left shoulder. The left hand is placed in the small of the performer's back and as the performer rolls backward and begins the push with the arms, the spotter lifts and assists the performer through the momentary hand balance. A spotter may be used at either side.

Dive Roll

Take several running steps and a low hurdle onto both feet, bounce from both feet, extend the arms, ride the hips high, and keep the head up until the hands contact the mat. As the hands contact the mat, bend the arms slowly while ducking the head and bending at the waist and knees. From this point, continue the roll to a standing position as described in the forward roll. The beginner's pike-dive roll is illustrated, but an arch dive might be learned eventually.

Safety: Use double thickness mats while learning and avoid contact with the head or neck unless such contact can be carefully controlled.

Cartwheel

From a stand with the legs a pace apart, raise the arms horizontally to the sides and shift the weight to the right, lifting the left foot slightly off of the ground. As you shift the weight back to the left side, bend at the waist and place the left hand about a pace away from the left foot. As the left hand moves to the mat, the right leg is raised and at the point of contact of the left hand to the mat, the left foot pushes from the floor. As the momentum carries the body weight onto the left arm, reach about shoulder width apart with the right arm so that the body weight is momentarily on both arms. At this point, the performer's position is a handstand with the head up and looking forward ahead of the hands. The back is slightly arched and the legs are straight and stretched wide apart. As the right hand contacts the mat, push with the left hand, then push with the right hand and bend at the waist, stepping down on the right foot. As the right foot comes to the mat, stretch the left leg and step down onto the left foot so that it is a pace away from the right foot. This should place the performer in the same direc-

tion and approximate stance that the stunt was started from. This stunt may be executed to the left or right.

Safety: A spotter may stand directly behind the performer and place his right hand on the performer's left hip and cross the left arm over so that the left hand is on the performer's right hip. As the performer moves to the left, the spotter moves too, lifting and assisting the performer through the correct position.

Cartwheel and Quarter Turn

This stunt is performed in the same manner as the cartwheel, except that as the right foot contacts the mat, the performer stretches the left leg and both arms while making a quarter turn on the ball of the right foot. As he makes the turn, the left foot steps out a pace, placing the performer in a good position to go into another stunt.

Safety: Same as for the cartwheel.

KIP-UP

From a sitting position, roll backward, piking at the hips and keeping the legs straight. Place the hands on the mat with the thumbs next to the ears and let the body weight rest on the hands and upper back. Hesitate when the knees come directly over the face and then immediately push with the hands and lash the legs upward, outward, then downward. This action should cause the head and shoulders to rise, allowing the performer to land in a standing position.

Safety. This stunt can be learned on the trampoline or with the help of a spotter. The spotter should take position beside the head and shoulders of the performer. If spotting on the right side, the spotter places the right hand on the performer's neck and the left hand at the small of the back. When the performer lashes upward and outward, the spotter lifts and assists.

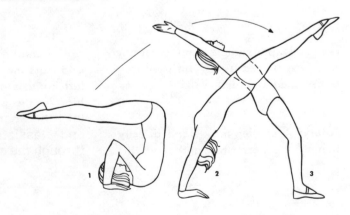

HEADSPRING

After taking several running steps and a low hurdle
from one foot onto both feet, squat and place the hands
on a rolled mat. As the feet push the body forward,
place the head a few inches in front of the hands and
allow the hips (piked position) to continue forward
until they are just past the vertical position. Then
push with the hands and extend the legs from the hips
upward, outward, and downward. As the head and
shoulders rise, the performer may land on the feet with
the back arched and legs straight, or with knees and
hips slightly bent. After the student masters this stunt
from the rolled mat, gradually decrease the height of
the roll until the skill can be performed without the aid
of the roll.

Safety. This stunt should be learned with the aid of a
rolled mat and with the assistance of a spotter. Spotting
on the right side of the mat, the spotter places the left
knee on the edge of the rolled mat and stretches the
right leg forward on the edge of the landing mat. The
spotter grasps the performer's right wrist with the left
hand and as the performer turns upside down, the
spotter's right hand lifts at the small of the back and
assists the performer to the feet.

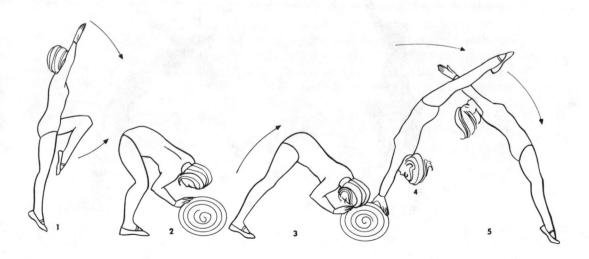

Handspring

Run forward on the mat and lift the left foot from the floor and skip on the right foot. After skipping on the right foot, place the left foot on the mat, bend at the waist, and place the hands a pace ahead of the left foot while keeping the arms straight and the eyes looking forward of the hands. Swing the right leg upward while pushing forcefully with the left foot. As the legs move upward through the handstand position, extend the shoulders and push with the hands and fingers. The back should be arched and as the head and shoulders rise, the performer should land on both feet with the legs straight or slightly bent, and the feet either even or separated into a walk-out position.

Safety: Same as for the headspring.

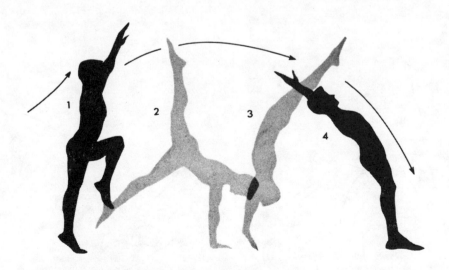

Forward Roll to Straddle Stand

From a stand, perform a forward roll and as the body weight gets on the upper back, split the legs wide apart and rush the roll onto the seat; driving the heels of the feet into the mat with force. As soon as the legs split, place the hands on the mat between the legs and as close to the crotch as possible. As the momentum from the roll carries you up onto your feet, push with the hands and lean the head and shoulders well forward. The legs should be kept straight throughout and the performer should complete the stunt in a wide-straddle stand or splits.

FRONT WALKOVER

Place the hands on the mat and kick upward with the right leg to a handstand with the legs in the split position. Arch over so that as the legs lower, the chest is pushed out over the arms to provide greater arch in the upper back. Land on the right foot, and at the same time push with the hands so as to assume a standing position on the right leg with the left leg stepping out well ahead of the right foot.

Safety. Standing on the right side of the performer as she kicks to a handstand, the spotter assists the performer over by placing the right hand under the hips as the left hand grasps the upper arm.

BACK WALKOVER

From a standing position with one foot ahead of the other, drop the head backward and go down slowly into a backbend. As the hands start to touch the floor, push upward with the lead foot and go through a handstand with the legs split wide apart and with the chest pushed forward over the hands. Return to the standing position by pulling the lead leg in as close to the body as possible. As the lead foot touches the floor, raise upward with the arms and step backward onto the other foot.

Safety. Standing on the right side of the performer as she bends backward, the spotter assists the performer over by placing the right hand under the hips as the left hand grasps the upper arm.

BALANCE AND
FLEXIBILITY SKILLS

Tripod Balance   From a squatting position, place the hands shoulder width apart with the fingers pointing straight ahead. Lean forward, bending at the elbows, and place the inside of the knees against and slightly above the outside of the elbows. Continue to lean forward until the feet come off the floor and the forehead rests on the mat. Balance in this position for as many counts as possible up to a maximum of 5 seconds.

Tip-Up

From a squatting position, place the hands shoulder width apart with the fingers pointing straight ahead. Lean forward bending at the elbows and place the inside of the knees against and slightly above the outside of the elbows. Continue to lean forward until the feet come off of the floor and balance on both hands with the face several inches from the floor.

Safety: If the performer overbalances forward, he should duck the head and perform a forward roll.

HEADSTAND

From a stand, bend forward and place the hands on the mat, shoulder width apart with fingers pointing straight ahead. Place the forehead—not the top of the head—on the mat several inches ahead of the hands. Keeping the body weight primarily on the hands, kick upward one foot at a time and maintain your balance with the back straight or slightly arched, legs straight and together, and toes pointed. To get out of this position, push with the hands, duck the head, and roll forward, or step down one foot at a time.

Safety. During the first few trials, as the performer kicks upward the spotter should be standing to the side and slightly to the rear in order to grasp the performer's legs and assist them to the proper position.

Head and Forearm Balance   Place the forearms on the mat and bring the hands close enough together for the thumbs and forefingers to form a cup to support the head. Place the back of the head in the cup formed by the thumbs and fingers, kick upward one foot at a time, and balance between the tripod support formed by the head and forearms. Balance in this position for as many counts as possible up to a maximum of 5 seconds.

Safety. Same as for the head balance.

Forearm Balance

From a kneeling position on one knee and one foot, place the forearms on the mat with the fingers straight ahead and slightly flexed. Kick upward one foot at a time and maintain a balanced position with feet overhead and with the head up and looking between the hands. The back should be slightly arched, legs straight and together, and the toes pointed. To get out of this position, duck the head and roll forward or bend at the waist and step downward one foot at a time.

Safety: Same as for the headstand.

Handstand

From a stand, bend forward and place the hands on the floor about shoulder width apart. The fingers should be spread apart and slightly flexed with the fingertips pressed against the floor and pointed straight ahead. Lean the shoulders over the hands and separate the feet so that one foot is ahead of the other. The head should be held up so that the eyes are looking forward of the fingertips. Swing the rear foot upward as you kick or push the near foot from the floor and maintain a balanced position with the feet overhead. This position should be maintained several seconds with the back straight or slightly arched, legs straight and together, and toes pointed.

A. There are several methods used to get out of this position. They are described as follows:

1. Step downward one foot at a time to the rear.
2. Overlean forward keeping the right hand in place and turn the head and shoulders to the right, causing the body to turn. The performer then merely separates the legs and steps down one foot at a time. The spotter should stand on the right side and place the right hand on the performer's left hip and the left hand on the right hip and turn the performer to the right.
3. Bend the elbows slowly, duck the head, and perform a forward roll back to the feet. In this method the spotter should grasp the ankles and lift them gently as the performer rolls forward. The spotter should release the grasp as the performer's back contacts the mat.

B. There are also several methods used to learn the handstand. They are described as follows:

Spotter and Wall Method

1. Place the hands about a normal step away from a wall and kick upward into a handstand with the assistance of a spotter. The distance from the wall will vary according to the individual. The spotter should assume a position to the side of the performer with one hand grasping the near shoulder and the other hand grasping the performer's near leg just above the knee. When the performer is secure against the wall, the spotter may remove his hand from the shoulder and use both hands in assisting the performer to maintain a free balance between the wall and the spotter's

hands. The performer should avoid ducking the head since it could result in a roll into the wall. The spotter and wall method is most often used to get the beginner started on the handstand.

Spotter Method

In this method, the spotter stands directly to the side of the performer and grasps the legs on the upward kick. When the performer is in the handstand position, the spotter releases the grasps on the legs and places one arm behind the legs, allowing the performer to maintain a free balance without letting an overbalance occur to the front or the rear.

Unassisted Method

This method is most commonly used when the performer has suc-ceeded in learning how to kick upward into position, hesitate, and get out of position safely. In this method, the performer works without assistance in attempting to maintain the balance on the hands. He learns to check or correct the balance by raising the head and pressing with the fingertips, shifting the body weight slightly to the rear when he is overbalancing forward; and to lower the head and lean the shoulders slightly forward, causing the body weight to shift toward the fingers when he is overbalancing to the rear. Learning the handstand takes some individuals much longer than others; however, the fastest way to develop a good handstand is to spend at least fifteen minutes a day working on it until you can consistently maintain this position for 3 or 4 seconds.

"V" SEAT POSITION

From a supine position, raise the legs and then roll slowly from the back forward onto the seat and hesitate for 3 seconds in a pike position with the hands grasping behind the legs or with the arms and hands extended horizontally to the sides. The legs should be straight and the toes should be pointed.

Front Scale

From a stand, lower the trunk forward so that it is approximately parallel to the floor and extend the left or right leg to the rear. Hold the head and chest high and arch the back while keeping the rear leg straight and raising it so that the foot is as high or higher than the head. Keep the supporting leg straight and hold the arms horizontally to the sides while holding the position for several seconds.

Side Scale

From a standing position, lean to the left side and lift the right leg until it is horizontal to the floor. The left arm is extended to the left and horizontal to the floor while the right arm is extended along the right side of the body with the hand resting on the thigh. The head may be held in its natural arc or it may be leaned close to the extended left arm. The supporting leg should be kept straight while maintaining the position for several seconds.

FRONT SPLITS

From a stand, slide the left or right foot forward, lowering the body downward until the crotch is within an inch of the floor. With one leg extended to the front and the other leg extended to the rear, maintain the splits position with the toes pointed, head up, and arms spread horizontally to the sides.

Side Splits

From a stand, slide the feet apart and to the sides lowering the body downward until the crotch is within an inch of the floor. The upper body faces forward and may be held upright or parallel to the floor. The arms should be extended horizontally to the sides.

"L" Position on Hands

From a sitting position on the floor, place the hands close to the sides of the hips and on the floor. Push with the hands by extending the shoulders, and lift the legs and seat from the floor. Keep the head up, chest out, legs straight, toes pointed, arms straight, and hold for several seconds. Some performers find it easier to slowly roll from the back forward onto the hands without letting the hips or legs touch the floor.

ROUTINE

Each student should be encouraged to create a free-exercise or tumbling routine using as many of the above stunts as possible.

POINTERS AND PROGRESSIONS TO PREVIOUS SKILLS.

1. The forward roll (p. 15) may be started from a squat or straddle stand position. This places the reluctant beginner closer to the floor for greater confidence.
2. The shoulder roll (p. 15) may be started from a kneeling position for reluctant students.
3. The backward roll (p. 16) may be started from a squat stand position to give greater momentum. Also the beginner may wish to maintain a tuck position throughout the roll, landing in a squat position until confidence and strength is developed for the extension upward.
4. The handstand position (p. 25) may give the impression that the back should be arched, however, as the beginner improves and holds the position longer, he or she should be encouraged to keep the back straight.

4

VAULTING SKILLS

GYMNAST DURING VAULTING PERFORMANCE

VAULTING TECHNIQUE

The beginner should learn to take a short, low hurdle on the beatboard from an abbreviated run before attempting any of the vaults below. The hurdle should not be used to get height, but merely to get both feet on the beatboard at the same time. In order to attain a reasonable amount of consistency, the performer should start from a predetermined distance measured from a desired spot on the beatboard. The performer should run fast enough to attain the necessary speed to perform the vault without sacrificing control. The eyes should be fixed on the beatboard at the start of the run and should remain there until a few feet before the hurdle is executed. Just prior to making the hurdle, the eyes should shift to the spot on the horse that the performer wishes to contact with the hands. The hurdle is made by jumping off one foot and landing both feet on the beatboard at the same time. The landing on the beatboard should be made on the balls of the feet, avoid landing flat-footed. The placing of the beatboard and the angle of the takeoff from it varies in accordance with the performer's physique and with the type of vault being executed. Following the desired vault over the horse, the performer should land on both feet with the knees bending naturally as the feet contact the mat and with the arms extending horizontally to the sides. Avoid taking extra hops or steps after the feet contact the mat.

SIDE-HORSE VAULTING

While side-horse vaulting (without pommels) is a competitive event for women, it is of the utmost importance in the teaching of vaulting to beginning male students in gymnastics. The beginner may profit from learning side-horse vaults and fundamentals of long-horse vaulting through the use of the side horse (with or without pommels). The following stunts are presented with the use of the pommels in mind. However, the pommels may be removed and the horse may be raised or lowered as the needs of the group or individual so indicate.

SQUAT STAND AND JUMP DISMOUNT

Run forward, take off from the beatboard with both feet, and reach for the horse. As the hands contact the horse, bend at the hips and knees, place the feet between the hands, and stand up on the horse. From the standing position, jump from the horse, stretch, and land on the feet with the back to the horse and the arms extended horizontally to the sides.

Safety. Have a spotter stand on the landing side of the horse to give assistance in the event that the performer's feet are improperly placed on the horse.

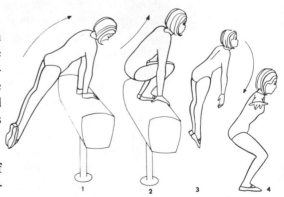

STRADDLE STAND AND JUMP DISMOUNT

Run forward and take off from the beatboard with both feet. Grasp the horse with both hands and, as the hips rise, lean on the hands, split the legs wide, pike at the hips, place the feet on the horse and stand up. From the straddle stand position, jump from the horse, close the legs, stretch, and land on both feet with the back to the horse.

Safety. Have a spotter stand on the landing side of the horse. If the performer leans too far forward in getting the feet on the horse, the spotter should grasp the arm and give support.

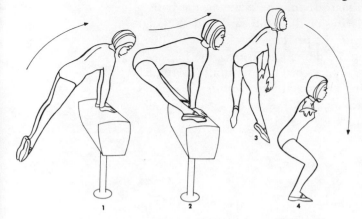

Front Vault

Run forward and take off from the beatboard with both feet. Grasp the pommels and turn the head and shoulders to the right while allowing the hips to rise and the legs to pass over the left end of the horse. The body weight should be on the right arm as the front of the body turns and faces the horse with the back arched. The left hand is released from the left pommel prior to the legs passing over the left end of the horse and is extended to the side as the performer lands on both feet with the right side nearest the horse. This vault may be performed to the left or right.

Safety: For those beginners who are hesitant to perform this stunt in the middle, move the beatboard to the neck section of the horse so that the beginner's legs pass over and beyond the end of the horse. Stress leaning on the right arm.

FLANK VAULT

Run forward and take off from the beatboard with both feet. Place both hands on the horse and lean on the right arm as you turn the right side of the body toward the horse. Release with the left hand and carry the legs over the left end of the horse. Release with the right hand and land on both feet with the back to the horse and the arms extended horizontally to the sides. This vault may be performed to the left or right.

Safety. Standing on the landing side of the horse, the spotter grasps the right wrist of the performer and assists, if necessary. This sunt may also be performed over the neck end of the horse.

Rear Vault

Run forward and take off from the beatboard with both feet. Grasp the pommels with both hands and as the hips rise, lean on the right arm and release the left hand as the legs pass over the left pommel and under the left hand. When the legs pass over the left pommel, regrasp with the left hand, release with the right hand, and land with the left side nearest the horse and the right arm extended horizontally to the side. This vault may be executed left to right.

Safety: Same as for the flank vault.

Straddle Vault

Run forward and take off from the beatboard with both feet. Grasp the pommels with both hands and as the hips rise, lean on the hands, split the legs wide, pike at the waist, push with the hands, and release. Keep the head up as the feet clear the ends of the horse. When the feet clear the horse, stretch the body, close the legs, and land on both feet with the back to the horse.

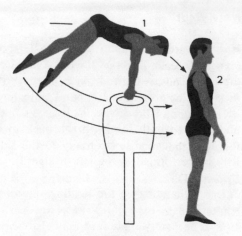

Safety: If possible, use two spotters on the landing side of the horse. As the performer releases with the hands, the spotters should reach forward and grasp the performer's arms and assist, if necessary.

SQUAT VAULT

Run forward, take off from the beatboard with both feet, and reach for the horse. As the hands contact the horse, bend at the hips and knees and push and release with the hands while the legs pass between the arms, in a squat position. As the push is made, raise the head upward and stretch the body prior to the landing. The landing should be made on both feet with the back to the horse.

Safety. One or two spotters may stand on the landing side of the horse and grasp the near arm as the performer executes the release.

Stoop Vault

Run forward and take off from the beatboard with both feet. Grasp the pommels with both hands and as the hips rise, lean forward on the hands, pike at the waist, push and release with the hands, and snap the legs between the pommels while maintaining a straight-leg position. As the feet clear the saddle of the horse, raise the head, chest, and arms (stretching) and land on both feet with the back to the horse.

Safety: Same as for the straddle vault.

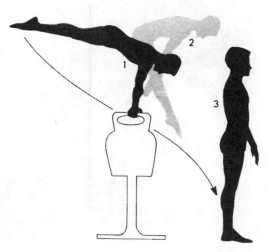

WOLF VAULT

Run forward, take off from the beatboard with both feet, and reach for the horse. As the hands contact the horse, push hard to gain height. As the body rises, tuck one leg over the saddle and extend the other leg over the end of the horse. As you clear the horse, bring both legs together, stretch the body, and land on the feet with the back to the horse.

Safety. Direct a spotter to stand on the landing side of the horse and to give assistance in the event that one of the feet does not clear the horse.

Thief Vault

Run forward taking off from the beatboard one foot at a time. Lift the leg up and through the pommels while pushing from the right leg. Immediately following this motion, draw the right leg between the pommels so that it joins the left leg. At this point, the legs are ahead of the body. As the hips rise over the pommels, place the hands on the pommels and give a quick push so that the head and chest will lift upward for the landing.

Safety: A spotter should stand to the side of the point of landing and be ready to assist the performer if the need arises.

STRADDLE VAULT WITH HALF TURN

Run forward and take off from the beatboard with both feet. Place the hands on the horse and, as the hips rise, lean on the hands, split the legs wide, pike at the hips, push with the hands, and start a turn to the right or left as the hands release. The head, shoulders, and arms should continue the initial turning movement from the hands until the half turn is completed. The landing should be made on both feet with the arms extended horizontally to the sides.

Safety. The spotter stands in the landing area and, in the event of difficulty, grasps the performer under the arms and supports her until the feet land. Otherwise, the spotter merely steps back out of the way as the performer lands.

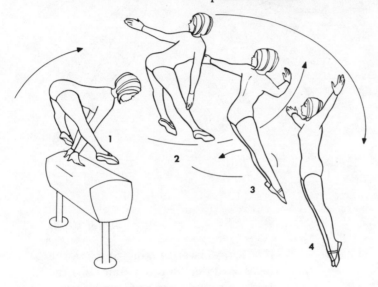

Headspring Vault

The headspring vault is performed in the same manner as the neckspring vault, except that the top of the head gently contacts the saddle instead of the back of the neck. In this stunt, the arms must exert a little more effort than in the neckspring.

Safety: Same as for the neckspring.

REAR VAULT WITH HALF TURN (INWARD)

This stunt is executed in the same way as the rear vault, except that the performer executes a one-half turn inward (toward the horse) so that the right side of the performer is next to the horse when the vault is executed to the left.

Safety. This stunt is not dangerous when the performer knows how to execute the rear vault. Therefore, learn the rear vault first.

Neckspring Vault

Run forward and take off on both feet while grasping the pommels with the hands. Pike at the waist and carry the hips high over the pommels. As the hips rise, the arms should bend and the head should be ducked under so that the back of the neck gently contacts the saddle of the horse. As the hips overlean toward the landing area, forcefully extend the legs forward (out of the pike position) and push and release with the hands. The landing should be made upon both feet while bending slightly at the knees and waist, and extending the arms horizontally to the sides.

Safety: Standing on the landing side and to the left of the performer, the spotter should grasp the left wrist while the performer's hand is on the pommel and use the right hand to assist in speeding up or slowing down the landing of the performer. The first few attempts at this stunt may be performed from a kneeling position on the horse or from a standing spring off of the beatboard.

FRONT VAULT WITH HALF TURN

Run forward and take off from the beatboard with both feet. Place the hands on the horse and turn the head and shoulders to the right while the hips rise and the legs pass over the left end of the horse. The body weight should be on the right arm as the front of the body turns and faces the horse; the back is arched. The left hand is lifted from the horse before the legs pass over the left end of the horse and it follows on around to take the supporting position as the right hand is lifted and turned to the outside. As the half turn is completed, the performer lands on both feet with the left side near the horse.

Safety. The spotter should stand on the landing side of the horse, facing the head and shoulders of the performer as she executes the move. If the performer has difficulty as she attempts to change supporting arms during the turn, the spotter should grasp her under the arms and support her until the feet land on the mat.

5

TRAMPOLINE SKILLS

JUDY WILLS SHOWS HER WINNING FORM AT THE WORLD TRAMPOLINE
CHAMPIONSHIPS, LONDON, ENGLAND

The rebound-tumbling or trampoline stunts described in this chapter are arranged in a simple-to-complex order; however, there is room for flexibility of arrangement. The authors suggest that students be encouraged to work quickly on trampoline stunts, taking about three or four tries at each turn on the apparatus with as few extra bounces as possible. Otherwise, a few students may monopolize the trampoline for the major portion of the class period.

Mounting the Trampoline

There are two methods which the performer may use to mount onto the trampoline properly. You may crawl on by using the hands and legs or by placing the hands on the frame, jumping the hips upward while ducking the head, and executing a forward roll into the middle of the canvas.

Dismounting from the Trampoline

There are many ways to get off a trampoline, but there is only one proper way for a beginner to do it. The beginner should place the right hand and the left foot on the frame. Keeping the weight on the right arm, step the right foot between the left foot and right arm and drop to the floor, bending at the knees on landing.

SPOTTING TECHNIQUE FOR HIGH ANGLE FALL   SPOTTING TECHNIQUE FOR LOW ANGLE FALL

Spotting Technique for the Trampoline

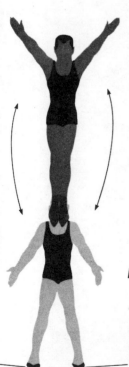

There should be one spotter for each of the four sides of the trampoline. If the performer is falling at a low angle toward the frame, the spotter should lean forward and push the performer back so that she does not contact the frame. If the performer is bounding from the trampoline at a high angle and it appears that she will miss the frame, the spotter should grasp the performer's arm or shoulder and step backward, allowing her to land her feet on the floor.

Proper-Bounce Technique

The performer should learn to place the feet apart when landing on the canvas and to keep the feet together while in the air. The arms should be raised on the ascent and lowered to the sides on the descent. The body should maintain an upright position while the eyes keep looking at the mat.

GYMNASTS SHOW WINNING FORM IN TRAMPOLINE EXHIBITION

TUCK BOUNCE

Bounce upward and draw the knees up to the chest by bending at the knees and hips. Grasp the shins with the hands and quickly release and straighten out for the descent.

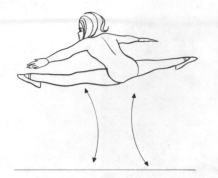

STRADDLE BOUNCE

This stunt is executed in the same manner as the pike bounce, except that the performer should split the legs as widely as possible while in the pike position.

Pike Bounce

Bounce upward and lift the legs so that they are straight and parallel to the canvas. Touch the shins with the hands and quickly straighten out for the descent. Be sure to lift the legs enough so that the upper body does not have to lean too far forward to touch the shins. The body should be bent only at the waist.

SEAT DROP

From an upright position, drop straight down to the canvas in a sitting position, so that the seat and the back of the heels contact the canvas at the same time. The head and shoulders should be maintained in an upright position and the hands should contact the mat on each side of the seat with the fingers pointing toward the feet. Push with the hands to return to the feet. Avoid jumping forward into a seat drop.

KNEE DROP

Keeping the body in an upright position, bend the knees at the peak of a bounce and drop to the canvas, landing on the knees, shins, and insteps. Avoid arching the back on this stunt since it could cause a strained back. To regain the feet, bounce from the canvas by raising the arms and by lifting the knees and toes off the mat together. The performer should try to avoid raising the knees early and riding back on the toes, for this may cause her to bounce backward out of control.

HANDS AND KNEE DROP

From a low bounce, tilt the upper body slightly forward and bend at the knees. Don't jump forward, but drop to the canvas so that the knees and hands contact the canvas together. The arms should be kept straight and the hands should contact the canvas in a direct line with the shoulders. To regain the feet, push with the hands, driving the head and shoulders upward while bringing the feet back in line under the body.

KNEE DROP-FRONT DROP

From a low bounce, perform the knee drop in the center of the canvas. As you rebound upward from the canvas, push the hips upward and backward, assuming a piked position. As you near the canvas again, stretch out of the piked position and land the beltline in the same spot that the knees had previously touched, to avoid a dive forward. In the landing position, you should be in a straight-prone position with the arms forward and elbows bent to the sides. The neck should be held rigid so that the chin will not contact the canvas. The hands, forearms, abdomen, thighs, knees, and insteps should contact the canvas simultaneously. To regain the feet, push with the hands and forearms, driving the head and chest upward and bringing the feet under the body.

FRONT DROP

This stunt is executed in the same manner as the knee drop-front drop, except that it is performed from the feet rather than from the knees. Remember to avoid diving forward on this stunt.

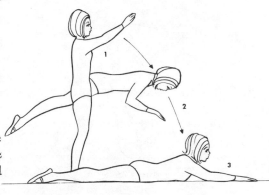

Back Drop

From a stand in the middle of the canvas, lift one leg upward, lean backward, and kick the other leg upward. As you drop to the canvas, pike at the waist with the eyes fixed on the knees. The hands should grasp the thighs or remain in an upward position. To regain the feet, bounce from the back while extending the legs outward and downward. To perform the back drop from a bounce, lift the legs and hips upward simultaneously and as the performer begins the drop to the canvas, he should follow the same procedure as described above.

Half-Twist to Front Drop

Bounce upward lifting the hips and legs as if going into a back-drop. Perform a half-turn by dropping the shoulder and looking in the direction that you wish to turn. As the turn is made, pike at the hips and hold the pike until the drop is almost completed. Just prior to contact with the canvas, extend the body for the front-drop position.

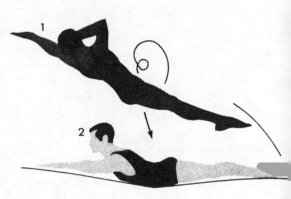

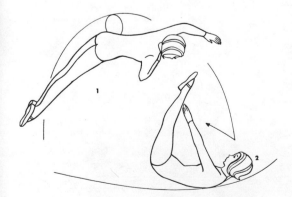

HALF-TWIST TO BACK DROP

Bounce upward and lean forward as if going into a front drop. Lower one shoulder and raise the other while looking in the direction of the lower shoulder. As you complete the twist, maintain a pike position, looking toward the knees, and perform the back drop.

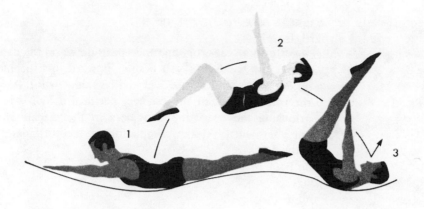

COMBINATION—FRONT DROP TO BACK DROP

Perform the front drop and, after landing, push hard
with the hands and forearms, thus driving the head and
chest upward and backward. As the head and chest
rise, bend at the knees and waist and continue to lean
backward until the back-drop position is achieved.

COMBINATION—BACK DROP TO FRONT DROP

Perform the back drop, and then kick upward and outward with the legs. As the head and shoulders rise and
the feet drop downward, maintain a pike at the hips
until just before contact with the canvas. To contact the
canvas, stretch the body out of the pike position and
land in the front-drop position.

SEAT DROP HALF-TWIST TO FEET

Perform a seat drop, and then push down on the canvas with the hands. As you bounce upward, lift the hands overhead and drive the feet and legs downward. As you reach the peak of the bounce, perform a half-twist by turning the head and shoulders in the direction you wish to turn. At the completion of the turn, land on the feet.

SEAT DROP HALF-TWIST TO SEAT DROP

This stunt is performed in the same manner as the seat drop half-twist to feet, but as the performer completes the half-twist, she bends at the hips and performs another seat drop.

BACK DROP HALF-TWIST TO FEET

Perform a back drop and then, kicking the legs upward and forward to raise the body, turn the head and arms to the left or right, completing a half-turn. At the completion of the turn, land on the feet.

BACK DROP HALF-TWIST TO SEAT DROP

This stunt is executed in the same manner as the back drop half-twist to feet, except that at the completion of the half-turn, the performer bends at the hips and lands in a seat-drop position.

BACK DROP HALF-TWIST TO BACK DROP

This is the same as the back drop half-twist to feet, except that at the completion of the half-turn the performer bends at the hips and leans backward, landing in another back drop.

ONE-HALF TURNTABLE

After landing in a front-drop position, push upward with the hands and knees and turn the head and shoulders either to the left or to the right. While the turn is being made, the feet and head should be low and the hips high. As the turn is completed, the performer stretches out of the pike or tuck position for the landing in the front-drop position.

FRONT SOMERSAULT

From a bounce in the center of the canvas, raise the arms and maintain them in an overhead position. As the feet again contact the canvas, bounce upward, pushing the hips slightly backward and swinging the arms and head downward. Tuck the chin to the chest, and tuck the body at the knees and waist with the hands grasping the shins. As the body rotates and nears the upright position, raise the head and open the body for a landing in the center of the canvas. Avoid leaning too far forward as this will cause you to land several feet from where you started. The performer should learn to somersault to the back and to the seat successfully before attempting to land on the feet.

BACK PULLOVER

Bounce upward, grasping the shins in a tight tuck position. As you drop to the canvas, the seat and feet should contact the canvas simultaneously. On the next upward bounce, pull on the shins and roll backward, keeping the chin tucked close to the chest. As the body nears an upright position, open up the arms and body and land on the feet.

ROUTINE

Combine as many of the above stunts as possible into a routine.

PART III

Events for Girls and Women Only

6

BALANCE BEAM SKILLS

The stunts for balance beam explained in this chapter are presented in a simple-to-complex progression. However, this particular sequence is arbitrary and is not meant to be inflexible. After assessing her individual interests and capabilities, the reader will be able to form her own order of learning. All of the stunts presented below may be learned with the beam at a low level and many of the stunts can be practiced on a line on the floor before the student tries them on the beam.

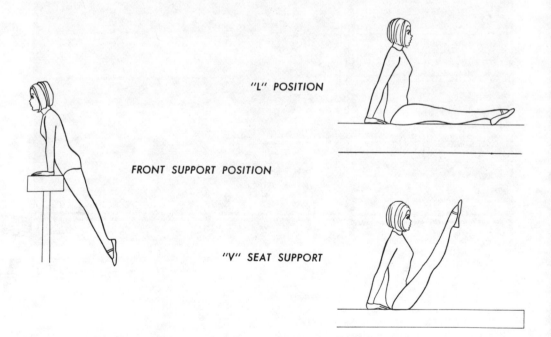

"L" POSITION

FRONT SUPPORT POSITION

"V" SEAT SUPPORT

FRONT SUPPORT MOUNT TO AN "L" POSITION

From a stand facing the side of the beam, place the
hands on the beam about shoulder width apart and
jump to a front support position, with the weight over
both arms and the hips or thighs leaning against the
beam. To complete the mount, swing one leg over the
beam to a crotch position. Move the hands to a rear
support as the legs come together and rest on top of
the beam in the "L" position or "V" seat support.

Safety. A spotter may stand by to assist the performer
in maintaining balance, if necessary.

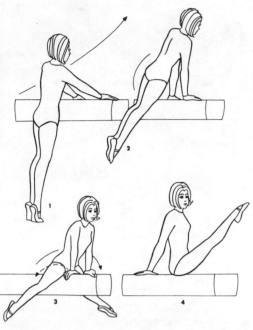

FENCE VAULT MOUNT

From a stand alongside the beam (left side near the
beam), take several running steps and lift the left leg
up and over the beam as the left hand pushes on the
beam. The right leg quickly follows the left leg over the
beam and the hands grasp the beam on each side of the
hips as the performer ends up in a side seat position.

Safety. A spotter should step in behind the performer
as she mounts the beam to steady her if she loses her
balance backward.

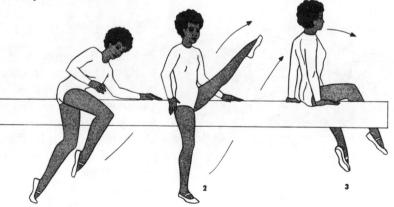

CROTCH SEAT MOUNT

From a stand alongside the beam (left side near the beam), take several running steps and lift the left leg upward as the left hand grasps the beam. Then move the right leg upward and the left leg down, pivot on the left hand by turning the head and shoulders to the left, and swing the right leg over the beam while keeping the left leg on the approach side of the beam. The right hand grasps the beam in front of the crotch as the turn is completed. Keep in mind that the action of the left leg is merely to move upward and then downward on the same side of the beam.

Safety.   A spotter may step in behind the performer (grasping the hips) and assist her on the turn to the crotch position.

PIVOT TO STAND FROM "L" POSITION

From an "L" position on the beam, flex the left leg so that the foot is on the beam and place the right hand behind the back and on the beam. Pivot to the right (keeping weight on left foot and right hand) while raising the hips upward and tucking the right leg under the body so that a half turn is completed. At the completion of the half turn the performer merely extends the right leg so that a standing position is achieved. Keep in mind that the left foot and right hand must rotate on the beam as the half turn is executed.

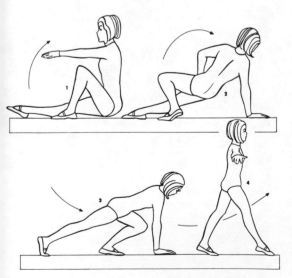

Safety.   This move may be performed on the floor several times before it is tried on the beam. A spotter may stand alongside the beam and give assistance if the performer loses her balance.

CAST TO KNEE SCALE AND RETURN TO STANDING POSITION

From a "V" seat position (hands supporting behind back) rock forward, splitting the legs on each side of the beam and grasping the beam in front of the crotch. As the body weight is transferred onto the hands, allow the legs to continue their swing to the rear. When the legs get above the beam, flex the right leg so that the knee and lower leg rest on the beam. Raise the left leg to a temporary scale position and then swing it downward and forward, placing the left foot between the hands and the right knee. Assume a standing position on the beam by extending the left leg and stepping forward on the right foot.

Safety.   A spotter may stand by to give assistance should the performer lose her balance.

SQUAT RISE FROM "V" SUPPORT

From a "V" seat support on the beam, roll the body forward, flexing the right leg and placing the right foot on the beam. The left leg maintains an extended position and swings downward alongside the beam. As the hands grasp the beam in front of the right foot and help the right leg extend the body weight upward, the left foot may be placed on the beam to the rear or may be allowed to swing forward to a step position.

Safety. A spotter should stand alongside the beam to help the performer get her weight over the right foot.

WALK

The walk on the beam should be graceful and slow. The toes of the nonsupporting foot should always be pointed as the foot swings around to the side and front for its next step. The arms should be held out to the side, but may move gracefully as the walk progresses.

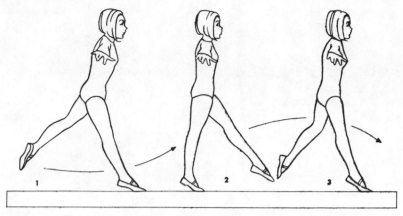

The eyes should focus near the end of the beam and not straight down.

Safety. The performer should practice the walk a few times on a line on the floor before getting on the beam. A spotter may assist the performer by holding her hand as she walks the beam the first few times.

STEP TURN

From a walk on the beam, step forward on the ball of the left foot and complete a half turn to the right, rotating on the balls of both feet as the head, shoulders, arms, and hips turn to the right. Avoid using the heels during the turn. During the turn the arms move to a curved position overhead and slowly open to the sides as the turn is completed.

Safety. The gymnast should practice the turn on a line on the floor before mounting the beam. A spotter may assist the performer during the first few trials on the beam.

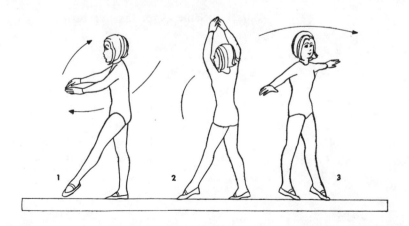

PIROUETTE TURN

From a walk, place the right foot on the beam and swing the left leg forward while turning right on the ball of the right foot. Lift the arms forward as the left leg swings forward and then turn to the right with the head, shoulders, and hips. As the turn is completed the left leg steps forward onto the beam. Avoid using the heel of the right foot during the turn.

Safety.   Same as for the step turn.

ARABESQUE TURN

From a stand forward on the left leg, shift the weight backward onto the right leg and swing the left leg in an extended position to the rear, completing a half turn to the left. The head, shoulders, arms, and hips assist the turn on the ball of the right foot by bearing to the left. At the completion of the turn the left foot is placed on the beam. Avoid using the right heel during foot rotation on the beam.

Safety.   Same as for the step turn.

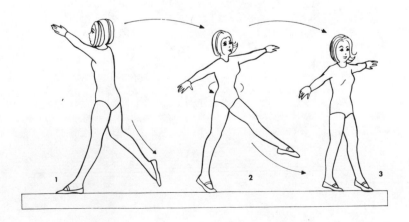

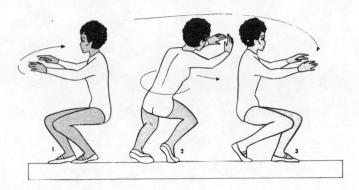

SQUAT TURN

From a standing position with one foot slightly ahead of the other, bend the knees until the seat is almost on the heels, and slowly pivot around to the opposite direction. The turn should be executed on the balls of the feet and the head, shoulders, arms, and hips should rotate in the direction of the turn. Avoid using the heels on the turn and when the turn is complete, return to a standing position.

Safety. Same as for the step turn.

SKIP STEP

From a walk on the beam, swing the left leg forward and, bringing the right foot up behind the left foot, perform a small jump. As the right foot again lands on the beam, the left foot quickly follows a pace ahead of the right foot.

Safety. This move may be practiced on a line on the floor before the performer mounts the beam. A spotter may stand by to give assistance when the stunt is performed on the beam.

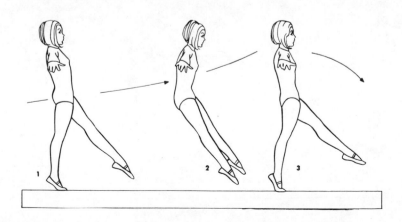

CAT LEAP

From a walk along the beam, step forward on the left foot, raise the flexed right knee, and leap from the left foot. As the left leg is flexed upward, step down on the right foot and quickly follow with the left foot, stepping forward. The arms should lift upward on the leap and open horizontally to the sides upon landing.

Safety. A spotter should stand to the side and be ready to assist if the performer loses her balance. The performer should practice this leap on the floor before trying it on the beam.

LEAP

The leap is made from one foot to the other foot while the performer executes a split in the air. In the jump from the right foot to the left foot, the right knee extends

from a slightly bent position while the left leg reaches forward. The landing on the left leg should be cushioned by bending the knee. During the leap, the toes should be pointed and the legs extended. Upon landing on the left foot, if the performer immediately steps forward on the right foot she will regain her balance easily.

Safety.   Same as for the skip step.

SQUAT LEAP

From a stand with one foot slightly ahead of the other, bend the knees until the seat is almost on the heels and jump upward, tucking the knees under the body. The arms should be lifted over the head and the trunk should be straight. Upon landing, the performer returns to the squat position.

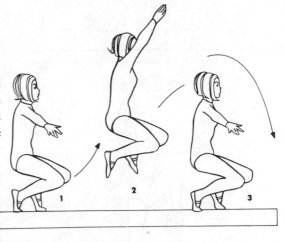

Safety.   Same as for the skip step.

SCISSOR LEAP

From a walk on the beam, step forward on the left foot and swing the extended right leg forward and upward as you leap from the left foot. As the right leg starts down for the landing, the extended left leg is lifted upward effecting a scissor action of the legs. As the right foot lands on the beam, the left foot follows and steps out a pace forward. The action of the arms is to lift upward on the jump and drop downward or horizontally outward to the sides on the landing.

Safety.   Same as for the skip step.

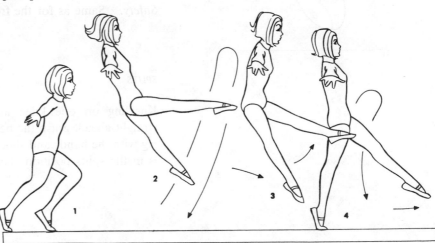

FRONT SCALE

From a stand on the beam, lower the trunk forward so that it is approximately parallel to the beam and extend the left or right leg to the rear. Hold the head and chest high and arch the back, while keeping the rear leg straight and raised so that the foot is as high as, or higher than, the head. Keep the supporting leg straight and hold the arms outstretched, and maintain the position for several seconds.

Safety. This stunt should be practiced on the floor before it is attempted on the beam.

ATTITUDE

Stand on the left leg and lift the right leg, bending the right knee and pointing the toes. The left arm should be curved overhead and the right arm extended out to the side.

Safety. Same as for the front scale.

"V" SEAT BALANCE

From an "L" position on the beam, bend the hips so that the legs are lifted upward and the trunk is rotated slightly backward. The arms should be extended horizontally to the sides or curved overhead as the performer balances with only the seat on the beam.

Safety. Same as for the front scale.

SPLITS

Kneeling on one knee and extending the other leg straight ahead, grasp the beam on each side of the front leg with the hands and slide the legs apart until the body is in the splits position. The hands may hold the beam

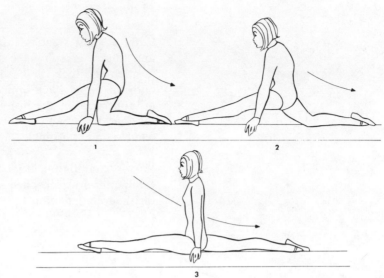

until balance is attained in the splits position. To get out of the splits position, release the back leg and swing it forward to an "L" position.

Safety.   First learn the splits on the floor and then use a spotter to assist you with balance when you perform the stunt on the beam.

STRADDLE-TOUCH DISMOUNT

From a stand at the end of the beam, jump forward and upward, lifting the legs to a side straddle pike position. Touch the shins with the hands and then straighten the body for the landing on the mat below. Be sure to lift the legs high enough so that the upper body does not have to lean too far forward to touch the shins.

Safety.   This stunt may be practiced on the floor and trampoline before it is attempted from the beam.

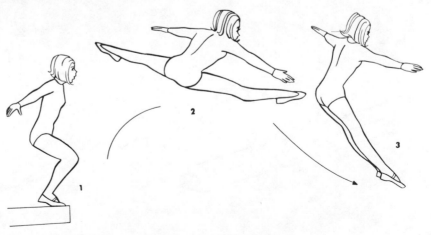

Forward Roll

From a squat stand with thumbs on top of the beam and fingers grasping the sides, lift the hips in a pike position and tuck the head under the body. Roll slowly onto the upper back and quickly change the hands to an undergrip on the beam while squeezing the elbows together. Continue the roll into a "V" seat balance or a one-leg squat position.

Safety: Standing in front of the head of the performer, the spotter grasps each side of the hips and assists during the rolling motion and shifting of the hands.

Back Shoulder Roll

From a back lying position on the beam, lean the head to one side and grasp under the beam as the legs are drawn over the body. Squeeze the elbows together as the legs are lowered to the beam. The roll is completed by placing one knee on the beam and shifting the hands to the top of the beam. It is usual to end in a knee scale.

Safety: Use a balance beam pad or folded towel while learning. The spotter should assist by lifting the hips and positioning the performer's knee to the beam.

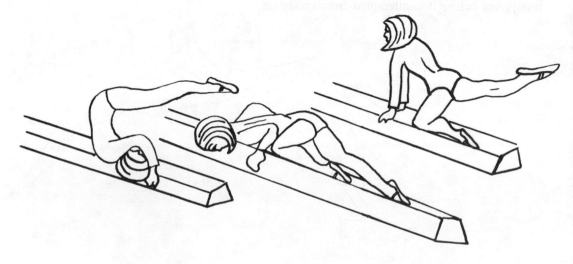

Backward Roll

Same as for the back shoulder roll except that the head remains on the beam and when the hands shift to the top of the beam, they push as the body turns to the rear.

Safety: Same as for the back shoulder roll.

FRONT DISMOUNT

From a stand, step forward on the right foot and lean to the front, placing the hands on the beam (wrist to wrist). As the hands reach the beam, kick upward three-quarters of the way to a handstand and shift the body to the right of the beam. At the landing, the left hand maintains contact with the beam while the right hand is extended horizontally to the right side.

Safety. A spotter should stand in the dismount area and grasp the performer's right wrist during the support phase of the stunt. As the performer lifts the right hand from the beam, the spotter assists her away from the beam by pulling outward. Also, a mat may be draped over the beam to give confidence to the performer.

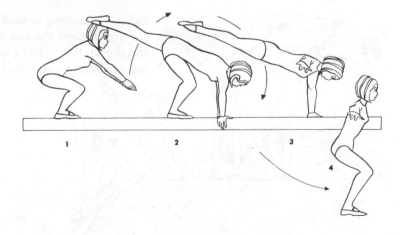

PIKE-TOUCH DISMOUNT

The technique is the same as for the straddle-touch dismount, except that the legs are kept together in a pike position. Remember that the body is bent only at the hips during the dismount.

Safety. Same as for the straddle-touch dismount.

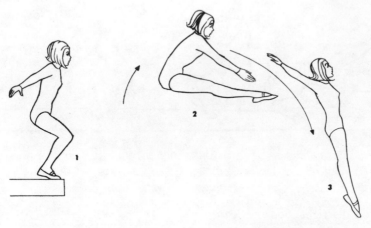

Roundoff and Cartwheel Dismounts

Standing near the end of the beam, the performer kicks the left leg upward placing the hands in an overgrip on the beam. The performer continues through a cartwheel motion bringing the legs together while pushing from the beam and doing a quarter-turn and landing on the mat facing the beam with both feet touching at the same time.

The cartwheel dismount is performed exactly as above except that the quarter turn is omitted and the performer lands sideways to the end of the beam, not facing it.

Safety: Standing behind the performer and grasping the arm nearest the end of the beam (above and below the elbow), the spotter assists the performer to her landing on either the roundoff or cartwheel.

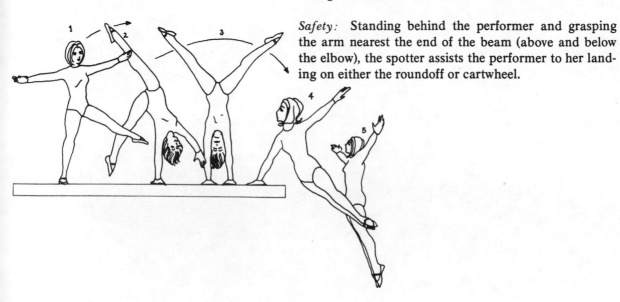

7

UNEVEN PARALLEL BARS SKILLS

The stunts for the uneven parallel bars, explained in this chapter, are given in a simple-to-complex order which may be considered somewhat flexible. Many of the stunts may be learned with the bars at a lower level than the height recommended for competition. The bars should be adjusted according to the difficulty of the stunt and the ability and desires of the students.

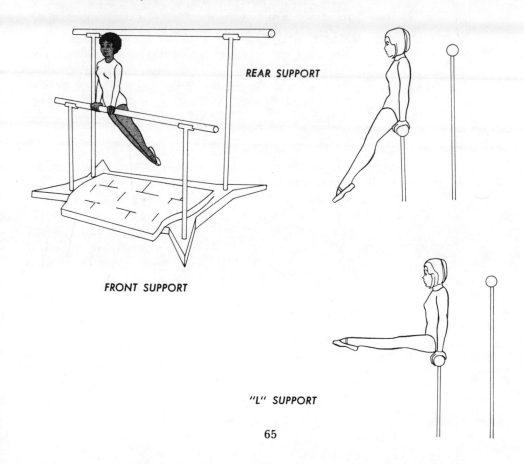

REAR SUPPORT

FRONT SUPPORT

"L" SUPPORT

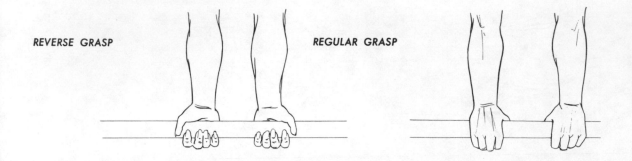

REVERSE GRASP   REGULAR GRASP

GERMAN HANG

Standing between the bars and with the back to the low bar, grasp the high bar and tuck the knees and hips (pulling body upward) between the arms and under the bar. Continue to extend the feet to the rear and downward until the insteps rest upon the low bar and steady resistance is met in the shoulders. At the completion of the stunt, return to the starting position.

Safety.   The performer should assume a piked position when passing the body between the arms and should keep the knees close to the trunk as she lowers downward.

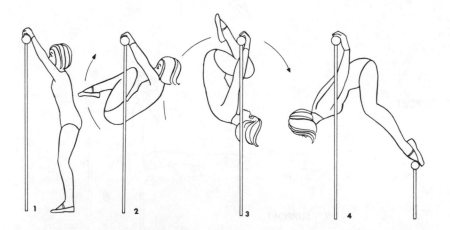

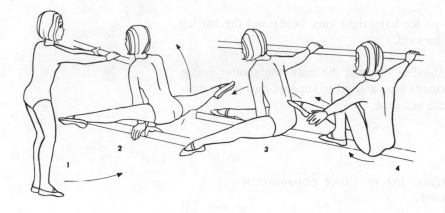

CROTCH SEAT MOUNT

From a stand on the outside of the bars (facing the low bar) assume a mixed grasp with the left hand under the bar and the right hand over it. Jump upward and swing the right leg over the low bar (supporting weight on the left hand) and release the right hand from the low bar to a regular grasp on the high bar. The stunt is completed in a sitting position with the left leg flexed (foot on the bar) and the right leg extended straight forward.

Safety. A spotter may grasp the performer's hips and assist her as she jumps and turns onto the low bar.

GERMAN HANG WITH SIMPLE TURN

Perform the German hang as described above, and as the insteps contact the low bar, release the right hand and turn the body under the left arm to a sitting position on the low bar. The stunt is completed with the

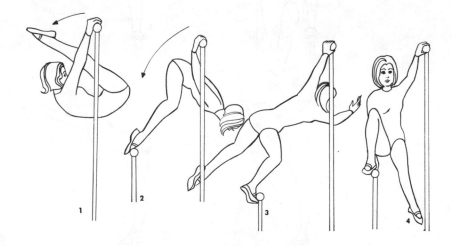

right foot on the bar (right knee bent) and the left leg extended forward.

Safety.   Standing between the bars, the spotter grasps the performer's hips and gives support during the one-hand release and turn.

ONE-LEG SQUAT RISE TO SIMPLE COMBINATION MOVEMENTS

From a sitting position on the low bar (right knee flexed and left leg extended forward beside the bar) and the left hand grasping the high bar with a regular grip, pull with the left arm and swing the left leg downward and backward as the right leg extends the performer into a scale position. From a scale position swing the left leg forward and up and over the high bar (from right to left), momentarily releasing the hands while the left leg passes over the bar, and finish up in a scale position facing the high bar.

Safety.   A spotter may stand by; however, there is very little danger of falling when performing this series of stunts.

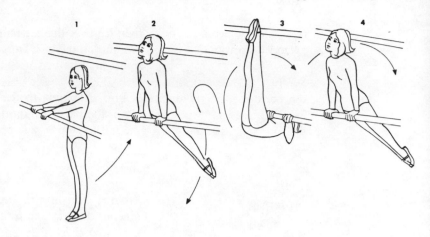

BACK PULLOVER MOUNT (LOW BAR)

Standing under the high bar and facing the low bar, grasp the low bar with a regular grip, jump the hips to the low bar, and allow the head and shoulders to rotate backward. As the body rotates, pull inward keeping the hips piked close to the bar until a front support is achieved.

Safety. Standing on the outside of the low bar and to the right side of the performer, the spotter reaches under the bar and grasps the performer's right wrist with the left hand turned so that the thumb is on the underside of the wrist and the fingers are on the top of the wrist. While the spotter's left hand is assisting the performer's grip rotation, the right hand assists the performer in keeping the hips close to the bar.

KNEE KIP-UP

Facing the low bar and using a regular grasp, pull the left leg between the arms and under the bar, and hook the knee over the top of the bar. Keeping the right leg straight, swing it forward and downward while pulling with the arms, thereby causing the body to rise above the bar in a support position. After mastering this stunt from a hang position, the performer should learn it from a swinging position by hooking the left leg over the bar, as the hips drop and swing forward, and then raising the body to a support position on the backswing. The performer may complete the stunt by bringing the

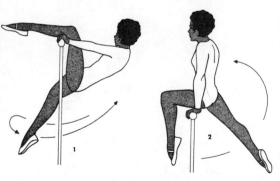

right leg over the bar and under the right hand to a seat position on the bar; from this position a variety of other stunts may be performed.

Safety. Standing to the side of the performer and between the bars, the spotter assists the performer should she fail to stop in a support on top of the bar.

SWAN

From a straight-arm support position on the high bar (facing the low bar) tilt slightly forward, holding the head and chest high, and arch into a swan position. As balance is gained, release the hands and extend the arms horizontally to the sides.

Safety. A spotter should stand below the high bar and be ready to give assistance should it be needed.

BACK PULLOVER MOUNT (HIGH BAR)

Standing under the high bar and facing the low bar, grasp the high bar with a regular grip. Draw the legs above the low bar and place the right foot on the bar while keeping the left leg extended forward. Push with the right foot and pull with the arms, causing the hips to rise toward the high bar. As the upper abdominal region contacts the high bar, the legs rotate over the bar and downward to the rear, causing the head and shoulders to rise above the bar. The stunt is completed in a straight-arm front support.

Safety. The spotter assists by placing one hand on the performer's near shoulder and the other at the small of her back and by pressing the performer upward during the pull and rotation phase of the stunt.

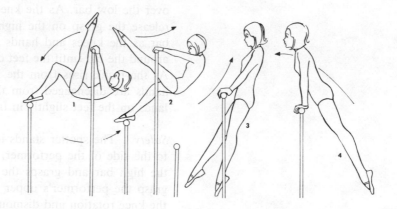

HELP-KIP

Starting with a regular grasp on the high bar (facing the low bar) and the right foot resting on the low bar, raise the extended left leg so that the shin is very near the top bar. At this point, pull with the arms, extend the supporting right leg, and force the extended left leg outward and downward so that the hips will rise and the performer will end up in a straight-arm front leaning position above the bar.

Safety. Standing under the bar and on the right side of the performer, the spotter may give assistance by placing the left hand on the performer's right thigh. As the performer kicks and pulls, the spotter pushes and assists her to a straight-arm support.

FORWARD ROLL FROM TOP BAR TO KNEE CIRCLE DISMOUNT FROM LOW BAR

From a straight-arm support with a regular grasp on the high bar (facing the low bar) roll forward, disengaging the hips from the top bar and hooking the knees

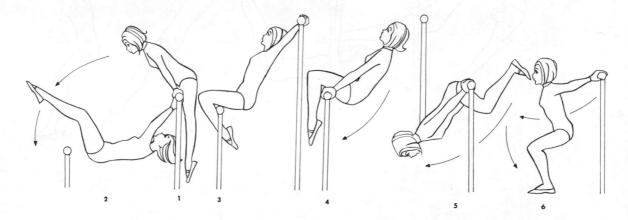

2   1   3   4   5   6

over the low bar. As the knees hook over the low bar, release the grasp on the high bar and regrasp the low bar as the knees and hands rotate backward half way around the bar until the feet can land on the mat below. As the trunk rises from the knee circle, the knees and hands are disengaged from the bar and the performer lands on the feet slightly in front of the low bar.

Safety. The spotter stands in front of the low bar and to the side of the performer. As the performer releases the high bar and grasps the low bar, the spotter may grasp the performer's upper arm and assist her during the knee rotation and dismount.

UNDERSWING DISMOUNT

From a straight-arm support above the high bar (back to the low bar) with a regular grasp, drop the shoulders backward and at the same time pike at the hips and pull with the arms, causing the feet to shoot upward and outward. At the completion of the pull, arch the back and push with the hands as you release the bar. The performer should land in a standing position.

Safety. Standing to the side and slightly forward of the bar, the spotter assists the performer in getting the hips high and steadies her on the landing.

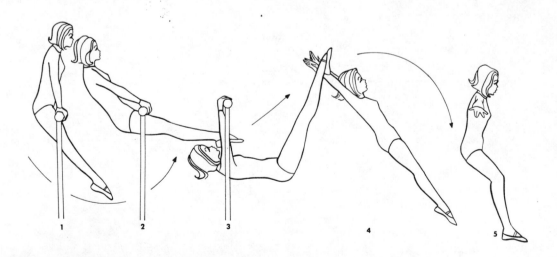

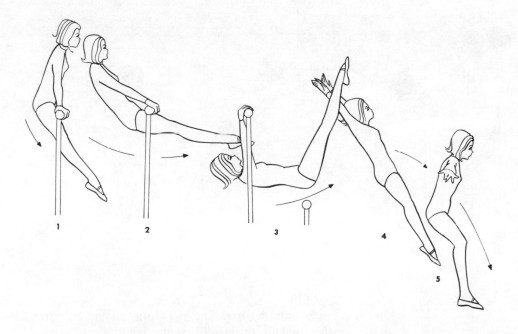

UNDERSWING DISMQUNT OVER THE LOW BAR

From a straight-arm support above the high bar (facing the low bar) with a regular grasp, perform the underswing dismount as described above, except pass over the low bar and land with the back to the bar.

Safety. Drape a mat over the low bar and have a spotter stand between the bars to assist the performer in getting the hips up and out for a clear landing beyond the low bar. A second spotter may be used in the landing area to steady the performer as she lands. As the performer develops confidence and skill, the mat may be removed.

UNDERSWING DISMOUNT AND QUARTER TURN
OVER THE LOW BAR

Perform the underswing dismount over the low bar as described above, but as the hands start to release, initiate a quarter turn left by turning the head and shoulders left. As the turn is completed over the low bar, grasp the low bar with the left hand and land with the left

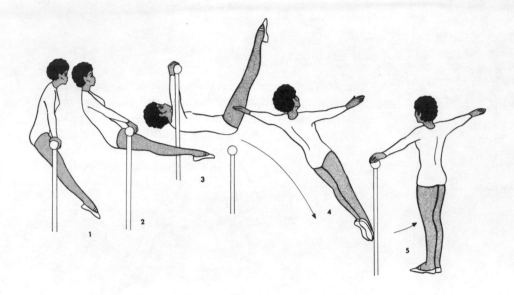

side near the bar. The right arm should be extended horizontally to the side at the landing.

Safety. Same as for the underswing dismount over the low bar.

UNDER BAR TURN

From a standing position on the low bar (facing the high bar), the hands grasp the high bar with a regular grip. Pushing the body under the high bar and releasing with the left hand, the performer turns inward around the right arm and regrasps the high bar with the left hand so that the hands are in a mixed grip position and the performer is facing in the opposite direction from her starting position. The left foot merely steps around to the opposite side during the turn, while the right foot pivots in place on the low bar.

Safety. Standing between the bars and to the right of the performer, the spotter places the left hand under the performer's right knee and gives support by turning under the high bar as the performer turns.

BACK HIP CIRCLE

From a straight-arm support above either the high bar or the low bar, lean slightly forward and push the hips backward away from the bar while arching the back. As the hips swing forward and contact the bar, pike and lower the shoulders backward, rotating the body around the bar by pulling inward and keeping the hips against the bar. ·

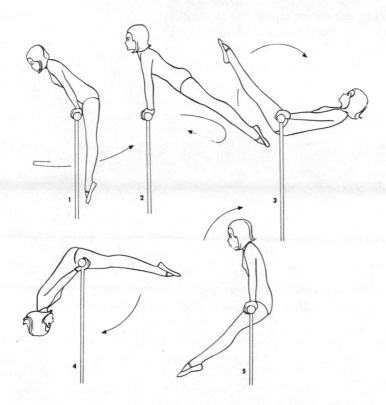

Safety. Standing on the opposite side of the bar and to the right side of the performer, the spotter reaches under the bar and grasps the performer's right wrist with the left hand turned so that the thumb is on the underside of the wrist and the fingers are on the top of the wrist. While the spotter's left hand assists the performer's grip rotation, the right hand assists the performer in keeping the hips close to the bar.

FORWARD HIP CIRCLE

From a straight-arm support above the low bar with a
regular grasp, pike slightly at the hips so that the upper
thighs rest against the bar. Roll the head and shoulders
forward (the neck should be extended so that the head
is well forward at the start) as fast as possible and slip
forward so that the abdomen, rather than the upper
thighs, is against the bar as the body rotates around the
bar. The hands may release the bar and grasp behind
the knees during the rotation so that the abdominal region and the forearms are resting on the bar as rotation
is almost complete. As the head and shoulders rise
above the bar, the hands regrasp the bar and the elbows
and the body are straightened to a straight-arm front
support position.

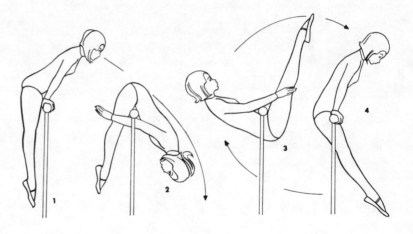

Safety.   As the performer rotates to the inverted position, the spotter may assist by pushing against the underside of the thighs, thus assisting the performer back to
a support position over the bar.

QUARTER-TURN DISMOUNT OVER LOW BAR
FROM HIGH BAR

From a front leaning rest on the high bar (facing the
low bar), lean forward and assume a mixed grasp on
the low bar (left hand under and right hand over). Let
the legs drop and then immediately whip upward, lifting the hips from the bar and shifting the weight onto
the hands. As the body passes through a handstand
position, release the right hand from the bar and execute a quarter turn to the left with the head and shoulders. The stunt is completed with the performer landing
on both feet with the left hand on the low bar and the
right arm extended horizontally to the side.

Safety. During the first few trials, use two spotters.
One spotter stands between the bars and helps the performer through the momentary handstand and over
the low bar, while the other spotter stands outside the
low bar and helps the performer to clear the bar by
pulling on the right arm after the right hand is released
from the bar. A mat draped over the low bar will provide additional protection for the performer.

FORWARD ROLL DOWN TO HALF TURN

From a front leaning rest on the high bar with a reverse
grasp (back to the low bar), pike at the hips and roll
forward to a hang below the high bar. Release the right
hand and the body will automatically complete a half
turn (right side of body rotating toward low bar). As
the turn is completed, regrasp the bar with the right
hand in a regular grip and immediately flex the hips and
place the feet on the low bar.

Safety. Standing directly behind the performer, the
spotter grasps the performer's hips and lifts as the need
arises during the release and rotation phase of the stunt.
The spotter turns with the performer in order to maintain a position directly behind the performer during rotation.

ROUTINE

Combine five or six stunts into a routine which is in
some way different from the routines of other members
of the class.

PART IV

Events for Boys and Men Only

8

HORIZONTAL-BAR SKILLS

The following stunts are explained in a simple to complex order, but may be considered as somewhat flexible. Many of the stunts may be performed with the bar low or high. Therefore, the bar should be adjusted in accordance with the nature of the stunt and the desires of the students. If the bar is lowered, it should be placed at about 4½ to 5 feet, and if raised, not above 8 feet.

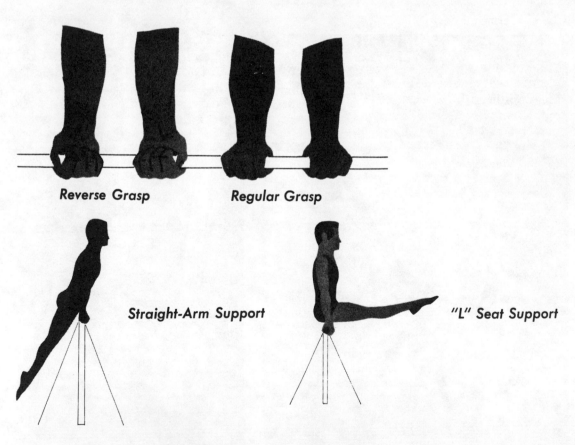

Reverse Grasp   **Regular Grasp**

Straight-Arm Support   **"L" Seat Support**

German Hang

Grasp the bar with a regular grip and while bending at the knees and waist, pull the legs upward between the arms and under the bar. Continue to extend the feet to the rear and downward until steady resistance is met in the shoulders. At the completion of the stunt, return to the starting position.

Safety: The performer should maintain a piked position with the knees close to the chest as he lowers downward.

German Hang—One Full Turn

This stunt is executed in the same manner as the German hang, except upon meeting a steady resistance in the shoulders, turn loose with the left hand and hang on with the right hand until a full turn has been completed. At the completion of the turn, re-grasp with the left hand. This stunt may be performed to the left or right.

Safety: Avoid a jerk in the right shoulder by making sure that both shoulders are fully extended before the release. A spotter may stand behind the performer grasping the hips and assisting the performer through the full turn.

Back Pullover

Using a regular grasp, pull the head and chest upward toward the bar with a chinning (flexing or pulling) action of the arms. Continue to pull with the arms while piking at the waist and raising the legs and hips upward over the top of the bar. As the upper-abdominal region contacts the bar, the feet lower downward to the rear, causing the head and shoulders to rise above the bar, finishing in a straight-arm support.

Safety: Standing under the bar and to the side of the performer, the spotter assists by pressing upward on the performer's shoulder as the hips and legs pass over the bar. The performer should avoid placing the lower-abdominal region against the bar since this will not allow enough body weight to the rear to cause the head and shoulders to rise smoothly.

Knee-Kip-Up

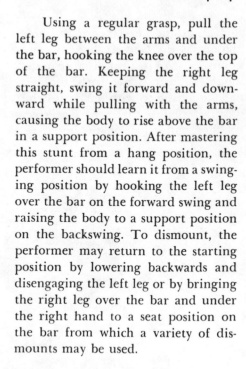

Using a regular grasp, pull the left leg between the arms and under the bar, hooking the knee over the top of the bar. Keeping the right leg straight, swing it forward and downward while pulling with the arms, causing the body to rise above the bar in a support position. After mastering this stunt from a hang position, the performer should learn it from a swinging position by hooking the left leg over the bar on the forward swing and raising the body to a support position on the backswing. To dismount, the performer may return to the starting position by lowering backwards and disengaging the left leg or by bringing the right leg over the bar and under the right hand to a seat position on the bar from which a variety of dismounts may be used.

Safety: Standing to the side of the performer and slightly forward, the spotter assists the performer should he fail to stop in a support on top of the bar.

Underswing Dismount

From a straight-arm support above the bar with a regular grasp, drop the shoulders backward and at the same time pike at the waist and pull with the arms, causing the feet to shoot upward and outward. At the completion of the pull, arch the back and push with the hands as you release the bar. The performer should land in a standing position.

Safety: Standing to the side and slightly forward of the bar, the spotter assists the performer in getting the hips high and in steadying the performer on the landing.

Underswing Dismount One-Half Turn

Same as the underswing dismount except that upon releasing the bar, the performer turns the head and shoulders to the right executing a one-half turn and lands facing the bar. The turn may be made to the left or right.

Safety: Same as for underswing dismount.

Pick-Up Swing and Simple-Back Dismount

Using a regular grasp, pull the body up toward the bar and at the same time pike at the waist, causing the feet to rise higher than the bar. When the feet attain this height, push with the arms, extending the legs upward and outward while arching the back. This enables the performer to obtain a good swing. As the body swings to the rear, pull with the arms and pike at the waist, letting the hips ride high. As the hips reach their peak, push downward on the bar, release, and straighten the body position for the landing.

Safety: Standing under the bar and to the side of the performer, the spotter should assist the performer in getting his hips up on the forward swing and maintain close hand contact with the performer until the downward push with the hands has been executed, in preparation for the dismount.

Kip-Up

Grasping the bar with a regular grip, swing forward and backward. As the body swings forward again, arch the back and at the peak of the forward swing quickly pike at the hips, bringing the insteps of the feet close to the bar. Maintain this piked position with the insteps near the bar until the hips swing backward between the uprights; extend the legs upward and outward as you pull and press the body above the bar with straight arms. The bar should remain close to the legs as they extend upward and outward. As the legs start downward, the hips should contact the bar smoothly. This stunt may also be learned with a reverse grip.

Safety: Standing under the bar and on the right side of the performer, the spotter may give assistance by placing the left hand on the performer's buttocks and the right hand on the back of the performer's right thigh. As the performer kicks and pulls, the spotter pushes and assists him to a straight-arm support.

Drop Kip

From a straight-arm support above the bar, the performer lowers backwards, piking at the waist and bringing the insteps of the feet close to the bar. Maintain this piked position with the insteps near the bar until the hips swing backward between the uprights. When the hips have passed the vertical uprights, kick the legs upward and outward and press the body above the bar in the same manner as demonstrated in the previous stunt.

Safety: Same as for the kip-up.

Back-Hip Circle

From a straight-arm support above the bar, lean slightly forward and push the hips backward away from the bar while arching the back. As the hips swing forward and contact the bar, pike and lower the shoulders backwards rotating the body around the bar by pulling inward and keeping the hips against the bar.

Safety: Standing under the bar (lowered for spotting purposes) and to the right side of the performer, the spotter grasps the performer's right wrist from the back side of the bar with the hand turned so that the thumb is on the under side of the wrist and the fingers are on the top side of the wrist. As the performer rotates around the bar, the spotter's right hand assists the performer in keeping close to the bar.

Forward-Hip Circle

From a straight-arm support above the bar with a regular grasp, slightly pike at the hips, causing the bar to rest against the upper thighs. Roll the head and shoulders forward (the neck should be extended so that the head is well forward at the start) as fast as possible while slipping the bar from the upper thighs to the abdominal region as the body rotates around the bar. Remember to keep the bar against the body throughout the stunt and slip the grasp, prior to the body leaning forward, into a support at the completion of the stunt.

Safety: As the performer rotates to the inverted position, the spotter may assist by pushing against the underside of the thigh, thus assisting the performer back to a support over the bar.

Circus Kip

From a hang below the bar with a regular grasp, develop a very slight swing, force the hips upward on the front swing, causing the back to arch. As the hips drop downward on the backswing, pike and forcefully pull with the arms, causing the body to snap upward into a straight-arm support above the bar. In the final phase, the pull of the arms transfers to a push. There should be no hesitation between the two.

Safety: Same as for the kip-up.

Back Up-Rise

From a hang below the bar using a regular grasp, cast the body upward and outward, developing a forceful swing to the rear. As the body gets directly under the bar, pull and continue the swing rearward while piking slightly at the hips. Prior to contacting the bar with the hips, the chest should be extended outward and the back arched. If the beginner is leery of contacting the bar with the hips, he may drop the shoulders as he nears the bar and perform a back-hip circle.

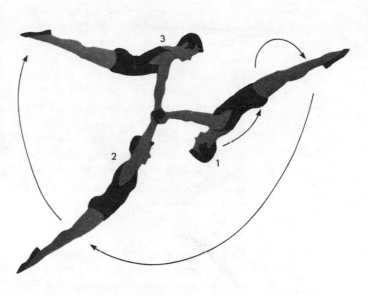

Safety: Standing to the side of the performer and slightly to the rear, the spotter may push on the performer's near leg, just above the knee, causing the hips to rise higher on the backswing.

Back Kip-Up

From a hang below the bar using a regular grasp, cast the body upward, outward, downward, and to the rear. As the body swings forward, ride the hips high and quickly pike at the hips, keeping the legs straight or bending at the knees, and bring the feet under the bar and between the arms. Maintain a tight pike, keeping the lower part of the legs close to the bar on the swing to the rear. As the swing forward begins, keep the legs and seat close to the bar by maintaining a steady pull while arching the back and lifting the head up. As the head, shoulders, and hips rise above the bar, slip the seat over the bar to a sitting position.

Safety: Standing to the side of the performer and directly under the bar, the spotter assists the performer by pushing under the hips as he arches the back and looks up.

Pike-Seat Rise

From a hang below the bar using a reverse grasp, cast the body upward, outward, downward, and to the rear. As the body swings forward, ride the hips high and pike quickly, bringing the feet under the bar and between arms. Maintain a tight pike as the body swings to the rear and pull with the arms, continuing the rearward swing until the body is over the bar in a seat position. Be sure and force the head and shoulders forward as the pull begins on the rearward swing and do not allow the back to arch.

Safety: Standing to the side of the spotter and directly under the bar, the spotter assists the performer by pushing under the hips as he begins his pike rise toward the top of the bar.

Back-Leanover Dismount

From a sitting position on top of the bar, drop the head and shoulders backward while arching the back and releasing the hands. Force the feet to remain on the forward side of the bar until they are whipped over by the tension of the arched back. The performer should land in a standing position below the bar.

Safety: Use two spotters if possible. One spotter insures that the feet remain on the forward side of the bar until the back is completely arched. The other spotter stands to the side of the performer and slightly to the rear of the bar. He supports the performer's near shoulder as he leans backward and releases the bar.

Routine

Combine five or six stunts into a routine which is in some way different from the routines of other members of the class.

9

PARALLEL BARS SKILLS

In the learning of parallel-bars stunts, the bars should be raised or lowered as the nature of the stunt and the needs of the individual dictate. The first sixteen of the following stunts may be learned with the bars set at a low level.

**Straight-Arm
Support**   **Straddle Support**   **Upper-Arm
Support**

Handwalk on Bars

From a standing position between the bars, jump to a straight-arm support and handwalk the length of the bars, keeping the legs together and the arms straight. Movement down the bars is achieved by leaning on one arm and stepping forward with the opposite hand. Take small steps with the hand and do not rush. This stunt emphasizes the importance of proper position and extension in movement.

Swing-Hop and Catch

From a straight-arm support between the bars, swing the legs forward causing the body to pike; at the same time hop forward by moving both hands simultaneously. As the hands regrasp, the legs swing downward and backward. Hop each time the legs swing forward. Do not bend the arms as the hop or catch is made.

Swing from a Straight-Arm Support

From a straight-arm support between the bars, lift the legs forward and extend the body into an arched position, allowing the legs to drive downward and backward. Lean slightly forward as the legs go to the rear and lean slightly backward as they move toward the front again. Do not let the elbows bend during the swing and remember that a good swing makes parallel-bar work easy.

Cross-Straddle Seat-Travel

From a straight-arm support between the bars, swing the legs forward causing them to split and rest on top of the bars. Lean the body forward, release the hands from behind, and regrasp the bars in front of the legs. Continue to lean forward, keeping the arms and legs straight, and lift the legs off of the bars, allowing them to swing forward again to the straddle-seat position. These movements may be repeated until the length of the bars has been traveled.

Front Dimount

From a straight-arm support between the bars, swing the legs forward, allowing them to drive downward and backward until they are well above the bars. As the legs reach their peak at the backswing, push with the right hand, causing the body to shift over the left bar. As the body begins its drop toward the mat, the right hand grasps in front of the left hand while the left hand is released and extended to the side. The right hand remains on the bar to steady the performer as he lands. This stunt may be executed to the left or right.

Safety: A mat may be draped over the left bar behind the left hand. Also, a spotter may grasp the left wrist of the performer and pull outward as the left hand is released.

Rear Dismount

Swinging from a straight-arm support, allow the legs to swing forward and reach a height slightly above the bars. Push with the left hand, causing the body weight to lean on the right hand. As the body is shifted over the right bar, the left hand releases the left bar and regrasps in front of the right hand on the right bar. The right hand is then released and extended to the side. The left hand remains on the near bar to steady the performer as he lands. This stunt may be performed to the left or right.

Safety: A mat may be draped over the right bar in front of the right hand. Also, a spotter may grasp the right wrist and pull outward as the right hand is released.

Front Dismount One-Half Turn

Swinging from a straight-arm support between the bars, allow the legs to reach a height well above the bars on the backswing. Push hard as you release the right hand, causing the body to shift over the left bar. The left hand is released momentarily as the thumb of the left hand is switched from inside the left bar to outside the left bar. As the left hand shifts to its new position, the body turns outward from the near bar, making a half-turn. The left hand remains on the left bar to steady the performer as he lands. This stunt may be performed to the left or right.

Safety: Drape a mat over the left bar behind the left hand so that the body makes its turn over the covered bar.

Rear Dismount One-Half Turn Inward

Swinging from a straight-arm support between the bars, allow the legs to swing forward slightly higher than the bars. Push hard as you release both hands, causing the body to shift over the right bar. As the body clears the bar, make a half-turn inward (toward the bar) and grasp the bar with the right hand to steady the landing. The left hand is extended to the side for balance. This stunt may be executed to the left or right.

Safety: Drape a mat over the right bar in front of the right hand so that the turn may be made over the covered bar.

Rear Dismount One-Half Turn Outward

Swinging from a straight-arm support between the bars, allow the legs to swing forward slightly higher than the bars. Lean to the left turning the head and shoulders over the left bar and at the same time pushing the right hand from the right bar. The left hand releases and immediately regrasps the left bar as the half turn is completed. This stunt may be executed to the left or right.

Safety: The spotter should stand to the side of the landing area and be ready to grasp the performer's right arm as he makes the turn.

Single-Leg Cut and Catch Mount

From a stand outside of the bars and facing the ends of the bars, grasp each bar and jump toward a straight-arm support. Before reaching the straight-arm support, split the legs and allow the right leg to pass over the right bar and under the right hand. Regrasp with the right hand and let the right leg drop between the bars while a straight-arm support is maintained. Be sure and lean on the left hand as the right hand is released and do not allow either arm to bend during the stunt. Students should learn the single-leg cut and catch using either leg.

Safety: Drape a mat over the right bar and immediately in front of the right hand. This allows the right leg to pass over a covered bar. Also, a spotter may stand behind the performer grasping the performer behind the belt (top of gym shorts) with right hand and lift as the performer jumps and goes through the stunt. The left hand supports the performer under the buttocks.

Single-Leg Cut and Catch (Center of Bars)

From a straight arm support in the center of the bars, the performer develops a low swing of the legs to the rear. As the legs reach a point slightly above the bars, cut the right leg over the right bar and under the right hand while releasing the right hand and vigorously leaning on the left bar. As the leg swings under the right hand, the performer regrasps the bar and passes his right leg in between the front bars to rejoin the left leg. This skill may be executed to the right or left.

Safety: Drape a mat over the right bar and immediately in front of the right hand. This allows the right leg to pass over a covered bar. Also, keep the bars at a low level while learning.

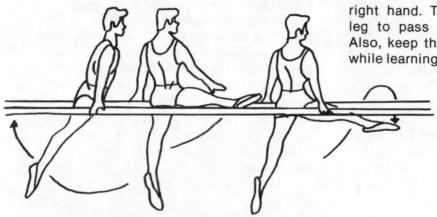

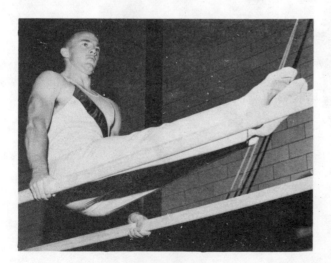

"L" Position

From a straight-arm support on the bars, the performer raises the legs until they are parallel and slightly above the bars. Avoid allowing the shoulders to sag or the back to round as the position is held for three seconds.

Safety: There is no danger in performing this skill, however, exercises for developing abdominal strength may be required as preliminary training.

Flank Cut and Catch Mount

From a stand outside of the bars and facing the ends of the bars, grasp each bar and jump toward a straight-arm support. Before reaching the straight-arm support position, lean on the left hand and allow both legs to swing over the right bar and under the right hand. Regrasp with the right hand and let the legs drop between the bars while a straight-arm support is maintained. Students should learn to flank to each side and remember that the arms should be kept straight throughout the sunt.

Safety: Same as for the single-leg cut and catch dismount.

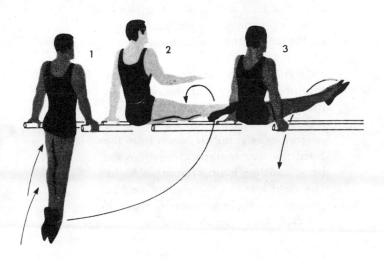

Straddle Cut and Catch Mount

From a stand outside of the bars and facing the ends of the bars, grasp each bar and jump toward a straight-arm support. Before reaching the straight-arm support position, push hard with both hands as the release is made and allow the legs to separate with each leg passing over the bar and under the corresponding hand. Regrasp with both hands and let the legs rejoin and drop between the bars as a straight-arm support is maintained.

Safety: Same as for the single-leg cut and catch dismount.

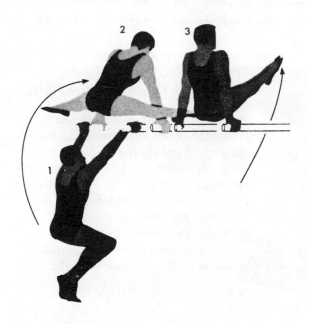

Straddle Dismount

Swinging from a straight-arm support between the ends of the bars and facing outward, allow the legs to swing backward until they reach a peak well above the bars. Allow the shoulders to lean slightly forward and push with the hands as the legs separate and pass over the bars and under the hands. The legs rejoin as the performer lands on his feet on the mat below.

Safety: Standing outside and slightly forward of the end of the right bar, the spotter grasps the performer's right wrist with the left hand. As the performer releases his hands from the bars, the spotter steps away from the bars, assisting the performer in flight. The right hand of the spotter may be placed on the performer's chest if difficulty occurs on the landing.

Flank Mount with Mixed Grip

From a stand outside of the bars facing the center of the near bar, place the right hand on the bar using a reverse grasp and the left hand on the same bar using a regular grasp. Jump, causing the hips and legs to rise higher than the bar, and at the same time lean the shoulders directly over the hands. The arms should be extending as the hips rise. Release with the left hand and while leaning on the right hand, turn the head and shoulders to the right, causing the body to turn and drop between the bars. As the body begins its turn over the near bar, regrasp the far bar with the left hand and swing between the bars. This stunt may be executed to the left or right.

Safety: Drape a mat over the near bar next to the left hand so that the body can turn over a covered bar.

Forward Roll in Straddle Position

From a straddle-seat position, grasp the bars in front of the legs and lean forward until the shoulders or upper arms contact the bars. With the elbows turned down to the outside, raise the hips until they lean slightly over the shoulders. Keeping the body in a pike position, release the grasp of both hands, crossing them on the lower part of the back to allow the roll to continue onto the arms until the performer reaches the straddle-seat position again. As the release is made with the hands, the performer must keep the elbows turned down to the outside, maintaining a straddle position with the legs.

Safety: Standing on the outside of the bars, the spotter places his right hand under the near bar with the palm of the hand against the performer's back. The spotter's left hand assists the performer in keeping the elbows turned downward.

Shoulder Stand

From a straddle-seat position, grasp the bars in front of the legs and lean forward until the shoulders or upper arms contact the bars. Keeping the elbows turned down to the outside, raise the hips until they attain a vertical position overhead. Holding the head up, extend the legs until they are directly overhead and together. At this point, assume a slight arch and point the toes. To get out of the shoulder stand safely, pike at the waist, separate the legs and lower to the starting position, or roll forward performing the straddle roll as described in the forward roll.

Safety: Same as for the forward roll.

Single-Leg Cut One-Half Turn

From a straight-arm support, swing the legs forward, crossing the right leg over the left bar while leaning on the left arm, and releasing the right hand from the right bar. At this point, the right hand grasps the left bar so that the right leg is between the left and right hands. The weight is now shifted to the right hand, and the right leg cuts under the left hand and back in between the bars as the left hand releases and then regrasps the opposite bar. The performer is now back in a straight-arm support, but facing in the opposite direction. Throughout the stunt, the left leg remains between the bars. This stunt may be executed to the left or right.

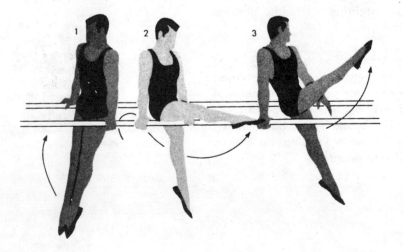

Back Uprise

From an upper-arm support, swing the legs forward and upward until the knees are piked approximately above the face. At this point, extend the legs forward and downward while maintaining a slight pike in the hips. At the bottom of the swing, drive the heels and hips backward into a forceful arch and pull hard with the hands, causing the feet to rise above the bars in the rear. As the shoulders move forward, the arms are extended into a straight-arm support position. During the swing downward and backward, do not allow the shoulders to sag between the bars since this slows down the swing.

Hip-Kip Straddle

From an upper-arm support, swing the legs forward and upward until the knees are piked approximately above the face. At this point, extend the legs forward and at the same time pull forcefully with the hands so that the head and shoulders rise as the legs separate and lower onto the bars. The stunt is completed with the performer in a straddle position on the bars with straight arms.

Safety: The spotter moves one hand under and between the bars placing it on the performer's buttocks while moving the other hand over the near bar and placing it behind the performer's neck. From this position he may assist the performer in the execution of the stunt.

Hip-Kip-Up

This stunt is performed in the same manner as the hip-kip straddle except that the legs remain together throughout the execution. This allows the performer to complete the stunt in a straight-arm support position.

Safety: Same as for the hip-kip strad-dle.

Drop Kip

With the hands on the ends of the bars, fingers curling over the bars toward the outside, jump slightly upward and pull with the arms (don't bend the elbows) so that the head and shoulders lean to the rear as the legs swing forward into a pike position with the knees over the face. Allow the body to swing forward while keeping the elbows straight. As the body swings backward, extend the legs upward and forward while pulling with the arms. The performer's head and shoulders should rise as the legs lower so that the stunt is completed in a straight-arm support. This stunt may also be performed in the middle of the bars by dropping back into a pike position from a straight-arm support above the bars.

Safety: By placing one hand on the buttocks and one hand on the back of the neck, the spotter may assist the performer in the execution of the stunt.

Routine

Combine five or six stunts into a routine which is in some way different from the routines of other members in the class.

10

RINGS SKILLS

In learning the following stunts, adjust the rings high or low in accordance with the nature of the stunt and the expressed desires of the students. Due to the weakness of the arms and shoulders of most beginners, it is recommended that the following safety techniques be observed closely.

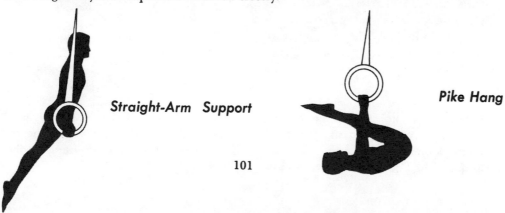

Straight-Arm Support

Pike Hang

101

Regular Grasp

False Grasp

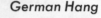

German Hang

Grasp the rings and pike at the waist, bringing the feet upward and over the head. Continue moving the feet from an over-the-head position downward until steady resistance is met in the shoulders. Keep the legs straight and toes pointed from the start. At the completion of the stunt, return to the starting position.

Safety: The spotter should assist the performer in getting his hips up and in maintaining a piked position. When strength and confidence improves, the spotter will not be needed.

Bird's Nest

Grasp the rings and pike at the waist, bringing the feet upward and between the rings. Engage the rings with the feet and arch the body below the rings until a steady resistance is met in the back. At the completion of the stunt, return to the starting position by ducking the head and bending at the hips.

Safety: A spotter should be on the alert and ready to assist should a weak student disengage his feet while in the arched position. In such a case, the spotter should grasp the performer's near arm just above the elbow and place the other hand on the chest.

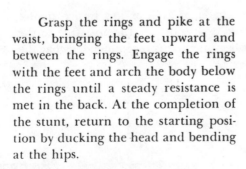

Inverted Hang

Grasp the rings and pike at the waist, bringing the feet upward between the straps. As the feet get between the straps, extend the legs and hips until they are directly overhead. This position should be maintained with the neck extended, body slightly arched, legs straight and together, with the toes pointed. Do not allow the elbows to bend while maintaining this balance. After holding for a few seconds, return to the starting position.

Safety: The beginner may rest his legs against the straps while maintaining the inverted position for the first few trials. A spotter may assist the performer in assuming the correct position by placing one hand on the performer's chest and one hand on the back.

Swinging To Tuck-Over Dismount

For this skill and other skills to follow, the performer must learn to swing on the rings from the hanging position. In developing the swing it is important to keep the center of gravity beneath the point of suspension. Thus, as the rings and feet swing forward, the hips swing backward; and when the feet and rings begin to move backward, the hips go forward. A good swing is de-

veloped by piking the hips on the forward swing and arching on the backward swing. In executing the tuck-over dismount from a swing, the performer merely bends at the hips and knees as he rides the forward swing upward and releases (turning over in the air) and lands on his feet below the rings.

Safety: Use a spotter on each side and grasp the performer's arms in the event of over-turning or under-turning.

Single-Leg Cut Dismount

Grasp the rings and pike at the waist, bringing the feet upward between and beyond the rings until the knees are directly over the face. Swing forward separating the legs, causing the left leg to return between the rings and the right leg to cut between the right ring and the right hand as the grasp is released with both hands. Prior to the release, roll the head and shoulders forward with a definite force. The performer lands on his feet with the arms extended to the sides for balance. This stunt may be executed to either side.

Safety: The spotter stands behind the performer placing the left hand on the back of the performer's neck and assists by pressing upward as the performer releases his grasp. The right hand of the spotter grasps the performer's waist to prevent an overthrow on the landing.

Single-Leg Straddle Dismount

Grasp the rings and swing the legs forward and then backward. As the legs swing forward again, pull with the arms and pike at the waist, causing the feet to rise well above the rings. Separate the legs, allowing the right leg to go between the straps and the left leg to pass between the left hand and the left ring as both rings are released. The head should be turned backward as the release is made to give the performer more momentum. As the performer lands on his feet, the arms should be extended to the sides for balance.

Safety: Standing on the right side of the performer, the spotter places his right hand on the performer's chest as the performer turns upside down and grasps the performer's upper arm with the left hand to prevent overturning.

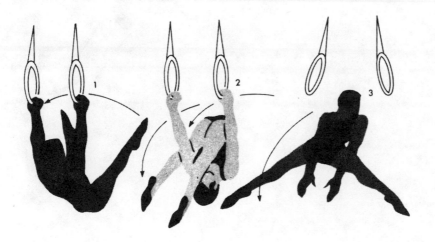

Double-Leg Cut Dismount

Grasp the rings and pike at the waist, bringing the feet upward between and beyond the rings until the knees are directly over the face. Swing forward separating the legs, causing the right leg to cut between the right ring and right hand and the left leg to cut between the left ring and left hand as the grasp is released with both hands. Prior to the release, the head and shoulders must roll forward with a definite force.

Safety: Same as for the single-leg cut dismount.

Double-Leg Straddle Dismount

This stunt is performed in the same manner as single-leg straddle dismount, except that as the legs separate the rings are pulled close together and both legs pass between the rings and the hands as the hands release. Remember to pull hard with the arms and turn the head backward to get enough momentum to land on the feet.

Safety: Same as for the single-leg straddle dismount.

Single-Leg Kip-Up

Grasp the rings and pike at the waist, bringing the feet upward between and beyond the rings until the knees are directly over the face. Forcefully roll the head and shoulders forward, causing the legs to separate and swing forward. The right leg passes between the rings driving outward and downward as the left leg hooks over the left wrist next to the left ring. The performer pulls with the arms and presses with the left leg as the body moves above the rings. After maintaining this position for a few seconds, return to the starting position. The pressing action of the leg may be executed to either side.

Safety: Standing on the right side, the spotter places the right hand on the performer's right knee as the right leg drives downward and pushes with the left hand under the buttocks.

Dislocate

Grasp the rings and pike at the waist, bringing the feet upward between and beyond the rings until the knees are directly over the face. Extend the legs backward while arching the back and keeping the arms straight.

As the legs extend to the rear, spread the arms and shoulders to avoid a jerk at the bottom of the swing.

Safety: If possible, for the first few times, use two spotters on this stunt. One spotter lifts on the chest while the other spotter lifts on the feet until the shoulders have dislocated.

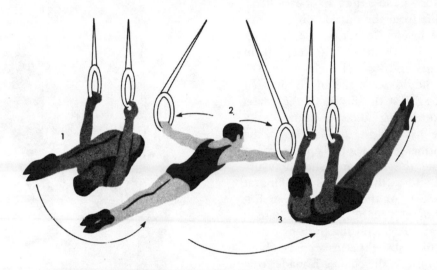

Inlocate

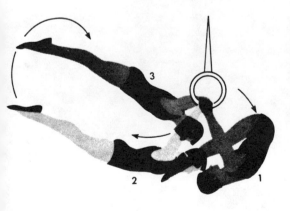

Grasp the rings, swinging the legs forward and then backward. As the legs reach their peak on the backswing, turn the rings inward while ducking the head forward and piking at the waist. The stunt is completed in a pike hang below the rings with the knees directly above the face. The first few tries may be made while standing on an object two or three feet high. The performer jumps, pushing his hips upward into the pike position while ducking the head and turning the rings inward.

Safety: As the performer's legs swing backward, the spotter, while standing on the right side, places his right hand on the performer's right hip and the left hand slightly above the perform-er's right knee. In this position, the spotter assists the performer in reaching his peak swing prior to the in-locate action of the shoulders.

Muscle-Up

Grasp the rings and while pulling the shoulders upward and bending at the elbows, cause the grip of each hand to shift from the outside of the rings to the inside. Do not release the rings with the thumbs, but keep them around the rings. This change of the grip should place the inside of each wrist against the inside of the corresponding ring. This is known as a "false grip." Using the false grip, the performer executes the muscle-up by pulling the head and shoulders upward and at the same time piking at the waist. As the shoulders lean forward over the hands, the arms cease to pull and begin on the push or extension to a straight-arm support above the rings. As the change is made from the pull to the push position, do not let the arms get wider than shoulder width apart.

Safety: Standing on the right side of the rings, the spotter places the right hand slightly above the right knee of the performer with the thumb on the underside. The left hand is placed on the underside of the right buttocks. As the performer pulls, the spotter pushes, assisting the performer in his first few efforts to get above the rings.

Double-Leg Kip-Up

Grasping the rings, using a false or regular grip, pull the legs upward until the knees are directly over the face. Push the legs upward and forward between the rings and at the same time pull with the arms. As the legs begin to drop downward, the head and shoulders rise above the rings in a straight-arm support.

Safety: Standing on the right side, the spotter places the left hand between the performer's shoulders and the right hand on the right buttocks. From this position, the spotter assists the performer to the straight-arm-support position.

"L" Position

From a straight-arm support above the rings, the performer pikes at the waist until the legs are parallel to the floor. In this position, the head is held erect, chest out, legs straight and together, toes pointed, and the rings are turned slightly outward away from the hips.

Safety: Learn to hold the "L" on the parallel bars before attempting it in the rings. Also, when first learning to perform on the rings, hold the rings close to the hips.

Single-Leg Front Lever

From an inverted hang below the rings, bend the right knee, placing the side of the right foot against the side of the left knee and lower the body until the back side of the body is parallel to the mat below. In this position hold the head back, chest up, back straight or slightly arched, and the left leg straight with the toes pointed. The position should be held approximately three seconds with the elbows straight.

Safety: Standing to the side of the performer, the spotter places one hand under the performer's hips and the other hand under the left knee, giving assistance to the performer until he develops the necessary strength to perform the stunt without help.

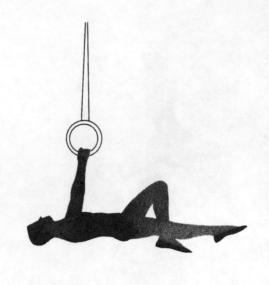

Beginner's Cross

Standing on a partner's shoulders, slip each hand between the canvas straps and grasp the lower part of the ring. Direct the partner to move and then lower into the cross position with the arms extending horizontally to the sides. The straps should support the forearms as the arms extend outward. After holding several seconds, direct the partner to again move under the rings for support.

Shoulder Stand

From a straight-arm support above the rings in the "L" position, bend at the elbows, allowing the shoulders to lower between the rings and the hips to rise between the straps. Keeping the head up, extend the legs overhead while turning the rings slightly outward, thus forcing the bent elbows next to the sides of the body. Keep the back slightly arched, toes pointed, and legs straight.

Safety: In learning the shoulder stand, separate the legs as the hips rise between the straps so that the back of the legs rest against the straps. With consistent practice, the performer should come to depend less and less on the use of the straps. Should the performer fall forward out of the rings, the spotter may slow the fall by pressing against the small of the performer's back.

Routine

Combine five or six stunts into a routine which is in some way different from the routines of other members of the class.

11

SIDE HORSE SKILLS

The following stunts for side horse are presented in a simple to complex progression. However, it should be noted that this particular sequence is arbitrary and is not meant to be inflexible. After assessing his individual interests and capabilities, the reader will be able to form his own order of learning.

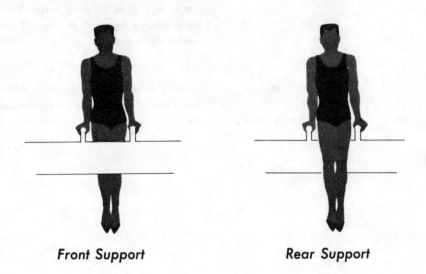

Front Support   **Rear Support**

Straddle Slide

From a front-support position with straight arms, lean on the right arm and swing both legs to the left, sliding the legs along the side of the horse. As the legs reach the peak of their swing, allow them to separate, causing the left leg to rise high above the horse. As the legs swing back, lean on the left hand and allow the legs to perform the same movement to the right. Perform this movement several times in succession to warm up the wrists and develop rhythm and proper lean.

Squat Mount to "L"

Grasp the pomels with both hands and jump the hips upward while extending the arms and shoulders and leaning forward. Bend at the knees and waist and pass the legs between the arms and over the saddle to a straight-leg bent-body "L" position. Hold this position for several seconds with the head up, legs horizontal to the floor, and toes pointed. Holding this position should contribute to the development of abdominal strength which is necessary for successful side-horse performance.

Feint Swings

From a front-support position with straight arms, shift the body weight on the right arm as you swing the right leg over the right end of the horse, thus straddling the right arm with the legs. From this position, swing the right leg back to the starting position, shifting the weight to both arms. Then lean on the left arm, and continue the left leg over the left end of the horse, straddling the left arm. Perform this movement several times to warm up the wrists, develop momentum, and improve proper lean.

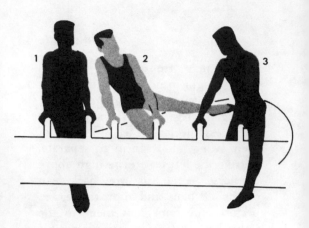

Single-Leg Half-Circles

From a front-support position with straight arms, swing the right leg over the right end of the horse while leaning on the left arm. As the weight is shifted to the left arm, the right leg passes under the right hand and over the right pommel to a position between the pommels. The weight is then shifted to the right arm as the left leg performs the same movement over the left end of the horse between and under the left hand to join the right leg in the center of the horse. As each leg passes under each hand, remember to regrasp, keeping the arms straight. Return to the starting position by swinging the right leg under the right hand and the left leg under the left hand, finishing in a straight-arm front support.

Single-Leg Full-Circle

From a front-support position with straight arms, lean to the right and swing the left leg over the left end of the horse. Release with the left hand and pass the left leg over the left pommel into the center. Regrasp with the left hand on the left pommel and lean to the left as the left leg continues its swing under the right hand and over the right end of the horse. Regrasp with the right hand as you return to the original position with straight arms. While the left leg is the center of attention as described above, the right leg remains on the approach side of the horse swinging to the left with the left leg, but returning to the right as the left leg cuts over the horse and continues to the right. This stunt may be performed to the left or right.

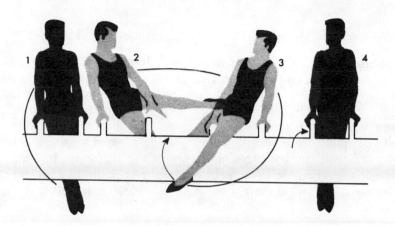

Double-Leg Half-Circles

From a feint position around the right arm, swing the legs to the left, passing them over the horse and between the left hand and the pommel. Regrasp with the left hand, keeping the arms straight, and stop in a straight-arm rear support. From this position, lean to the left and swing the

legs over the right pommel and under the right hand, returning them to the approach side of the horse. As the legs clear the right pommel, regrasp with the right hand and return to a straight-arm front-support position. This stunt may be performed to the left or right.

A helpful hint to note in executing this stunt is that as the regrasp is made with the right hand, lean slightly forward with the right shoulder and keep the right arm straight; otherwise, the performer will not be able to finish in a straight-arm front support.

Double-Leg Half-Cut Mount to Single-Leg Half-Circles

From a stand with the hands on the pommels, jump while leaning on the right arm and cut both legs between the left hand and left pommel. As the left hand regrasps the left pom-mel, lean on the left arm and cut the right leg between the right hand and and right pommel. As the right hand regrasps the right pommel, perform the same movement to the left with the left leg. The stunt is completed with the performer in a straight-arm front-rest position. This stunt may be performed to the left or right.

Single-Rear Dismount

From a front support with the left hand on the neck of the horse and the right hand on the left pommel, feint around the right arm. From this position, lean on the right arm and swing the legs over the left end of the horse and under the left hand. With the left hand regrasp the end of the horse, release with the right hand, and land on both feet with the left side nearest to the neck of the horse. On the landing, the right arm should be extended horizontally to the side. This stunt may be performed to the left or right.

Single-Leg Travel

From a front-support position on the pommels with straight arms, swing the right leg over the right end of the horse while leaning on the left arm. With the weight on the left arm, the right leg passes under the right hand and over the right pommel to a position between the pommels. The weight is then shifted to the right arm as the

left leg swings over the left end of the horse. The body weight is then shifted back to the left arm as the left leg comes to rest next to the left hand and left pommel. The performer's legs are at this point straddling the left hand and left pommel. As the right leg swings between the right hand and right pommel in order to move over

the right end of the horse, the right hand is shifted to the left pommel and in front of the left hand. As the right leg clears the right end of the horse, the left leg swings back over the left end of the horse and the left hand is shifted to the end of the neck section. This stunt may be executed to the left or right.

Double-Rear Dismount

With the hands on the pommels, attain a feint position with the legs straddling around the right arm. Keeping the body weight on the right arm, swing the right leg around the croup so that it joins the left leg and lift the left hand from the left pommel so that the legs can swing over the pommel and continue toward the croup. The head, shoulders, and hips should turn to the right so that when the legs clear the end of the croup, the left hand can

rest on the end of the croup. At this point the right hand is released from the right pommel, the feet land on the mat with the left side closest to the croup, and the right arm is extended horizontally to the side. This stunt may be performed to the left or right.

Safety: As the performer's right leg joins the left leg from the feint position, a spotter may step in and grasp the right wrist with the right hand and the left hip with the left hand and thus assist the clearing of the end of the horse as well as the landing.

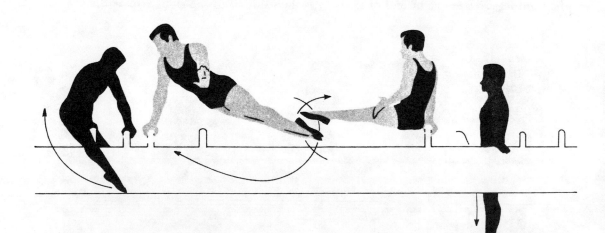

Front Scissors

From a straight-arm support with the right leg between the pommels and in front of the horse and the left leg in back of the horse, swing the legs to the left as you lean on the right arm. When the legs near the peak of their swing, release with the left hand and cross the right leg under the left leg. As the legs cross, they separate and return downward with the left leg to the front and between the pommels and the right leg to the back. The left hand regrasps as soon as the crotch passes between the pommels. This stunt may be executed to the left or right.

Safety: For the first few trials, the performer should place the feet on the left end of the horse with the left hand still between the legs and on the pommel. As the performer slides the right leg under the left leg, he should release with the left hand, complete the scissors of the legs, and regrasp as the crotch passes into the center between the pommels. This method instills confidence and thereby facilitates the process of learning the scissors.

Rear Scissors

From a straight-arm support with the left leg between the pommels and to the front and the right leg in back of the horse, swing the legs to the left and lean on the right arm. When the legs near the peak of their swing, release with the left hand and cross the right leg under the left leg. As the legs cross, they separate and return downward with the right leg to the front and between the pommels and the left leg to the rear. The left hand regrasps

the right hand. As the performer be-
comes more adept, he should strive to
start the mount from a position facing
the neck section with the right hand
on the left pommel and the left hand
on the end of the neck.

Safety: A spotter may stand behind
the performer grasping his belt with
the left hand and placing the right
palm under the right buttocks. As the
performer jumps, the spotter lifts,
turns, and assists the performer into
the completed position.

Hop-Turn Travel (From Saddle to Croup)

From a straddle support in the
saddle, with the right leg in front and
the left leg in the rear, lean on the
right arm as the left leg cuts under
the left hand. As this cutting action
takes place, press the back of the right
leg against the saddle and hop to the
end section of the horse. While executing the hop, both legs should come
together and the lean should continue

to the right until the legs have passed
over the end of the horse. The stunt is
completed with the left hand on the
end section, the right hand still on the
pommel, and the legs between the
hands. The stunt may be performed to
the left or right.

Safety: From a position facing the
performer, a spotter may step forward and give assistance after the
legs of the performer meet and start
toward the croup.

Routine

Combine five or six stunts into a
routine which is in some way different from the routines of other members of the class.

APPENDIXES

B

PHYSICAL PRINCIPLES OF GYMNASTICS

PHYSICAL PRINCIPLES INVOLVED IN GYMNASTICS

A few of the scientific principles involved in executing beginning skills in gymnastics are listed as follows:

1. Static balance is directly proportional to the area of the base on which the body is supported.

   Example: Greater stability is gained in the handstand position if the fingers are spread well apart.

   Example: When bouncing on the trampoline, the performer should land on the bed with the feet a pace apart, as opposed to the feet together, so that greater stability can be obtained.

2. The static balance of a body is indirectly proportional to the height of the center of gravity of that body above its base.

   Example: In executing a straddle or pike-touch dismount from the beam, it is important for the performer to lower the body's center of gravity by bending the knees upon contact with the mat. Bending the knees also aids in absorbing the shock of the dismount (by spreading the force of the landing over a distance).

   Example: To make a steady landing from a side-horse vault, it is important for the performer to lower the body's center of gravity by bending the knees upon contact with the mat.

   Example: In making a steady stop from a high bounce on the trampoline, bend the knees and waist as you contact the bed. This lowers the center of gravity and kills the spring by spending the force of the landing over a distance.

128

3. In support stunts, the center of gravity of the body should fall as nearly as possible over the point of support (the hands, arms, or feet).

> *Example:* In performing a front scale on the beam, the performer maintains the center of gravity directly over the supporting foot as the trunk rotates forward and the non-supporting leg rotates backward.

> *Example:* In the stoop vault over the horse, the center of gravity moves in the direction of the vault and the stoop between the arms is executed at the peak of the lift above the horse.

> *Example:* In the tip-up position on the hands, the center of gravity falls at a point directly between the hands.

> *Example:* In side-horse skills, the center of gravity is held over the supporting hand by leaning the shoulders in one direction as the hips move in the opposite direction.

> *Example:* In swinging from a straight arm support on the bars (un-evens, parallel bars or horizontal bar), the shoulders should lean forward as the feet swing to the rear and vice versa as the feet swing forward.

4. To absorb the shock of a fall, the shock should be spread over as large a body area as possible and as long a distance as possible.

> *Example:* If a headspring or handspring is overturned, the performer should extend the arms, wrists, and fingers and relax gradually, giving in upon contact with the mat (spreading out the shock) rather than landing on the face or chest.

> *Example:* Bending the knees and the hips upon landing from dismounts, aids in absorbing the shock of the landing (by spending the force of impact over a distance).

5. The moment of force may be reduced by keeping the center of weight as nearly as possible under the point of support.

> *Example:* In the German hang, the hips should assume a tight pike (with the knees close to the trunk) as the legs rotate between the arms and downward. If the hips and legs are allowed to extend to the rear, the center of weight may be thrown far enough from the point of support (the hands) to snap the performer loose from the bar.

6. In pressing body weight, the center of gravity should fall as nearly as possible over the point of support. This reduces the effort necessary to raise the body.

13.   In skills where horizontal distance is needed, maximum speed should be attained at the moment of takeoff.

> *Example:* In performing vaults over the side horse, the gymnast should not slow down the run prior to takeoff. Failure to observe this principle causes many beginners to land on the horse rather than on the mat on the other side of the horse.

14.   In mounting stunts which involve swinging or rotary movement, the center of gravity should be brought as close to the center of support or of rotation as possible at the crucial movement.

> *Example:* In performing the help-kip, keep the center of gravity as close as possible to the center of rotation (the hands). Failure to comply with this principle creates a moment of force in which the center of gravity cannot be shifted over the hands as the head and shoulders rise.

15.   In swinging activities, decreasing the radius of rotation on the swing upward will accelerate the movement while increasing the radius on the downswing increases the linear velocity of the center of gravity at the bottom of the swing.

> *Example:* This may be accomplished by swinging on the still rings from a hang, flexing the hips and elbows at the start of the upswing, and extending the hips and arms at the beginning of the downswing.

16.   In the basic drop stunts, the center of gravity must be directly over the point at which the feet left the trampoline.

> *Example:* This principle is basic to such stunts as the seat, knee, back, and front drops on the trampoline.

17.   The height to which the vaulter rises above the horse depends upon the amount the beatboard is depressed, the angle of takeoff (lean), and the push of the hands (in some instances) on the horse.

> *Example:* The effects of each of the named factors can be seen in the execution of a straddle vault over the side horse.

18.   The height to which the performer rises above the trampoline depends upon the amount the bed is depressed and the angle of takeoff.

> *Example:* This principle is illustrated by the difference in height attained during a straight vertical jump and a front somersault. Since some lean is needed for the somersault, the performer cannot attain maximum height in this stunt.

19. All essential turning movements start as the body leaves its point of support.

> *Example:* To execute a forward somersault, there must be some lean forward to get the center of gravity ahead of the feet on takeoff in order to produce the necessary rotation.

20. The law of falling bodies governs all non-aerodynamic objects and is based on the pull of gravity whereby such objects accelerate downward at the rate of 32 ft. per second/per second.

> *Example:* When more time for somersaulting and/or twisting is desired, the gymnast should strive for greater height to gain time for completion of movement.

	Lower Limit	Average	Upper Limit
18. Back Drop 1/2 Twist to Back Drop	4.00	4.50	5.00
19. One-half Turntable	4.00	4.50	5.00
20. Front Somersault	4.00	4.50	5.00
21. Back Pullover	4.00	4.50	5.00

BALANCE BEAM

	Lower Limit	Average	Upper Limit
1. Front Support Mount to "L" Position	2.00	2.25	2.50
2. Fence Vault Mount	2.75	3.00	3.25
3. Crotch Seat Mount	3.25	3.50	3.75
4. Pivot to Stand from "L" Position	3.00	3.25	3.50
5. Cast to Knee Scale and Return to Stand	2.75	3.00	3.25
6. Squat Rise from "V" Seat Position	3.50	4.00	4.50
7. Walk	1.00	1.25	1.50
8. Step Turn	2.00	2.25	2.50
9. Pirouette Turn	3.00	3.25	3.50
10. Arabesque Turn	2.00	2.25	2.50
11. Squat Turn	2.25	2.50	2.75
12. Skip Step	2.00	2.25	2.50
13. Cat Leap	3.00	3.50	4.00
14. Leap	3.75	4.25	4.75
15. Squat Leap	3.50	3.75	4.00
16. Scissor Leap	3.75	4.25	4.75
17. Front Scale	2.75	3.00	3.25
18. Attitude	2.25	2.50	2.75
19. "V" Seat Balance	2.25	2.75	3.25
20. Splits	4.50	4.75	5.00
21. Straddle-Touch Dismount	4.00	4.25	4.50
22. Pike-Touch Dismount	4.00	4.25	4.50
23. Front Dismount	3.25	3.50	3.75
24. Forward Roll	4.00	4.50	5.00
25. Back Shoulder Roll	4.25	4.50	4.75
26. Backward Roll	4.00	4.50	5.00
27. Roundoff or Cartwheel Dismount	4.00	4.50	5.00

UNEVEN BARS

	Lower Limit	Average	Upper Limit
1. German Hang	2.25	2.50	2.75
2. Crotch Seat Mount	3.00	3.25	3.50
3. German Hang with Simple Turn	3.25	3.50	3.75
4. One-leg Squat Rise and Combination Movements	1.50	1.75	2.00
5. Back Pullover (Low Bar)	3.25	3.50	3.75
6. Knee Kip-up	3.50	3.75	4.00
7. Swan Balance	2.75	3.00	3.25
8. Back Pullover (High Bar)	3.50	3.75	4.00
9. Help-Kip	3.75	4.00	4.25
10. Forward Roll to Knee Circle Dismount	3.00	3.25	3.50

		Lower Limit	Average	Upper Limit
11.	Underswing Dismount	3.75	4.00	4.25
12.	Underswing Dismount over Low Bar	4.00	4.25	4.50
13.	Underswing Dismount 1/4 Turn over Low Bar	4.25	4.50	4.75
14.	Half Turn from Low Bar to High Bar	1.75	2.00	2.25
15.	Back Hip Circle	4.00	4.25	4.50
16.	Forward Hip Circle	4.00	4.50	5.00
17.	Forward Roll Down 1/2 Turn to Low Bar	3.50	3.75	4.00
18.	Quarter-Turn Dismount over Low Bar	4.00	4.50	5.00

HORIZONTAL BAR

		Lower Limit	Average	Upper Limit
1.	German Hang	1.25	1.50	1.75
2.	German Hang-Full Turn	2.50	2.75	3.00
3.	Back Pullover	3.00	3.25	3.50
4.	Knee Kip-up	3.00	3.25	3.50
5.	Underswing Dismount	3.25	3.50	3.75
6.	Pick-up Swing and Simple Back Dismount	3.25	3.50	3.75
7.	Kip-up	4.00	4.50	5.00
8.	Drop Kip	4.25	4.50	5.00
9.	Back-Hip Circle	4.00	4.25	4.50
10.	Forward Hip Circle	4.25	4.50	4.75
11.	Circus Kip	4.50	4.75	5.00
12.	Back Up-rise	4.00	4.50	5.00
13.	Back Kip-up	4.50	4.75	5.00
14.	Pike Seat Rise	4.50	4.75	5.00
15.	Back Leanover Dismount	4.25	4.50	4.75
16.	Underswing Dismount One Half Turn	4.25	4.50	4.75

PARALLEL BARS

		Lower Limit	Average	Upper Limit
1.	Cross-Straddle Seat Travel	1.00	1.25	1.50
2.	Front Dismount	3.00	3.25	3.50
3.	Rear Dismount	3.00	3.25	3.50
4.	Front Dismount-Half Turn	4.00	4.25	4.50
5.	Rear Dismount-Half Turn	4.25	4.50	4.75
6.	Single Leg Cut and Catch	3.50	3.75	4.00
7.	Flank Cut and Catch	4.50	4.75	5.00
8.	Straddle Cut and Catch	4.50	4.75	5.00
9.	Straddle Dismount	4.00	4.25	4.50
10.	Flank Mount	4.00	4.25	4.50
11.	Forward Roll in Straddle Posit.	3.75	4.00	4.25
12.	Should Stand	4.25	4.50	4.75
13.	Single Leg Cut-Half Turn	4.25	4.50	4.75
14.	Back Uprise	4.00	4.25	4.50
15.	Hip-Kip Straddle	3.75	4.00	4.25

		Lower Limit	Average	Upper Limit
16.	Hip-Kip-up	4.00	4.25	4.50
17.	Drop Kip	4.50	4.75	5.00
18.	Single Leg Cut & Catch (Center of Bars)	4.50	4.75	5.00
19.	"L" Position	4.00	4.25	4.50

STILL RINGS

1.	German Hang	.75	1.00	1.25
2.	Bird's Nest	.75	1.00	1.25
3.	Inverted Hang	1.00	1.25	1.50
4.	Single Leg Cut Dismount	3.00	3.25	3.50
5.	Single Leg Straddle Dismount	3.00	3.50	4.00
6.	Double Leg Cut Dismount	4.00	4.50	5.00
7.	Double Leg Straddle Dismount	4.00	4.50	5.00
8.	Single Leg Kip-up	4.25	4.50	4.75
9.	Dislocate	4.50	4.75	5.00
10.	Inlocate	4.50	4.75	5.00
11.	Muscle-up	4.00	4.50	5.00
12.	Double Leg Kip-up	4.50	4.75	5.00
13.	"L" Position	4.00	4.25	4.50
14.	Single Leg Front Lever	4.50	4.75	5.00
15.	Beginner's Cross	4.50	4.75	5.00
16.	Shoulder Stand	4.50	4.75	5.00
17.	Swinging To Tuck-Over Dismount	3.75	4.00	4.25

SIDE HORSE

1.	Squat Mount to "L"	2.25	2.50	2.75
2.	Feint Swings	2.00	2.25	2.50
3.	Single Leg Half Circles	3.00	3.50	4.00
4.	Single Leg Full Circle	3.25	3.75	4.25
5.	Double Leg Half Circles	3.50	4.00	4.50
6.	Double Leg Half Cut Mount to Single Leg Half Circles	4.00	4.25	4.50
7.	Single Rear Dismount	3.75	4.00	4.25
8.	Single Leg Travel	4.00	4.25	4.50
9.	Double Rear Dismount	4.00	4.50	5.00
10.	Front Scissors	4.00	4.50	5.00
11.	Rear Scissors	4.00	4.50	5.00
12.	Beginner's Baby Moore	4.50	4.75	5.00
13.	Baby Loop Mount	4.25	4.50	4.75
14.	Hop Turn Travel	4.50	4.75	5.00

Additional Reference:

Teas, Charles. *Common Gymnastic Skills in Compulsory Routines.* Un-published Listing. Del Mar College, Corpus Christi, Texas, 1976.

INDEX